PENN & TELLER'S
HOW TO PLAY IN TRAFFIC

FROM THE AUTHORS OF
Cruel Tricks for Dear Friends
How to Play with Your Food

PENN & TELLER'S
HOW TO PLAY IN TRAFFIC

BY
PENN JILLETTE AND TELLER
THE AUTHORS OF <u>HOW</u> <u>TO</u> <u>PLAY</u> <u>WITH</u> <u>YOUR</u> <u>FOOD</u>
Design by Robert Bull / Photographs by Anthony Loew

BOULEVARD BOOKS, NEW YORK

Photograph p. 131 Lambert/Archive Photos
Photograph p. 227 New York Public Library Picture Collection

PENN & TELLER'S HOW TO PLAY IN TRAFFIC

A Boulevard Book / published by arrangement with
Smokin' Monkey Productions, Inc.

PRINTING HISTORY
Boulevard trade paperback edition / November 1997

The Putnam Berkley World Wide Web site address is
http://www.berkley.com

ISBN:1-57297-293-9

BOULEVARD
Boulevard Books are published by The Berkley Publishing Group,
a member of Penguin Putnam Inc., 200 Madison Avenue,
New York, New York 10016.
BOULEVARD and its logo are trademarks
belonging to Berkley Publishing Corporation.

PRINTED IN THE UNITED STATES OF AMERICA

10   9   8   7   6   5   4   3   2   1

DESIGN AND INTERIOR PRODUCTION BY ROBERT BULL DESIGN

DEDICATION

Mam Teller, Mom Jillette, Dad Jillette, and Pad Teller — the four best parents who have ever lived. Some of this book is opinion — the previous sentence is fact.

CONTENTS

STORIES —
REALLY TRUE AND KINDA TRUE.

STUPIDLY EASY TRICKS —
JUST READ 'EM AND DO 'EM.

JUST AS STUPIDLY EASY TRICKS — BUT MAYBE YOU HAVE TO STICK SOMETHING IN YOUR POCKET.

REAL TRICKS — IT'S NOT GOING TO HURT YOU TO LEARN SOMETHING.

HARD, IMPOSSIBLE, IMMORAL, AND/OR ILLEGAL TRICKS — MAYBE YOU'LL GO TO JAIL.

INTRODUCTION —
Judging Our Book by Its Cover

WHAT CAN YOU LEARN FROM THE COVER OF *Penn & Teller's How to Play in Traffic?* The title and the passport motif should clue you to the travel theme. If you want to be a little more enlightened, go the extra half mile (it *is* a travel book) and judge the book by the front cover, back cover, *and* table of contents — you could learn even more.

On the back cover we advertise a comparison between Motel 6 and The Plaza. If you look at our multifunctional table of contents, you'll see no mention of The Plaza or Motel 6. As a matter of fact, a computer search would tell you that the words "Motel 6" and "Plaza" don't appear anywhere in the book unless you count the back cover, this sentence, the two previous sentences, Motel 6 without The Plaza in the parenthetical following this sentence, the two sentences one sentence after that, the two sentences that are three sentences after that (with another two Motel 6 and three The Plaza mentions in the parentheses), the closing salutation, and the four Motel 6 mentions without The Plaza. (There's one really in the book, albeit in passing, on page 40, one five words from here, and the two other Motel 6 mentions in the last paragraph of this introduction.) We considered changing the one on page 40 to "fleabag motel," just to make them come out even (because we would cut the two in the *QEII* paragraph as well) but why would that matter to anyone? That's thirteen references to The Plaza and seventeen references to Motel 6 — quite a few — but all those (except the one in passing in the body of the book and that's only one) are a little too self-referential to really count. And where are you going to find the entire text of our whole book on computer for this theoretical Motel 6 / The Plaza search? By the time you scan it in, you could have found this introduction and page 40 yourself. Especially now that we told you where to look.

The discrepancy between the information on the cover and the contents of the book just proves we're experts on travel. We were so busy traveling that when the deadline for the cover copy snuck up on us we didn't remember that we'd already cut out Penn's bit about Teller's detective work on the Motel 6's $.50 TV keys because it was a stinker and they no longer use those TV keys anyway. (We don't really know how The Plaza got mentioned on the back cover to begin with. Maybe the publisher people stuck it on — but we can't figure why. They wouldn't get free rooms at The Plaza for their other authors by saying Motel 6 is better than The Plaza on the cover of our book, and we doubt the publisher wanted free rooms at Motel 6 for their other authors — you know how other authors are about lodging.) So, Motel 6 and The Plaza stayed on the back cover without being anywhere in the book except this introduction and, of course, the back cover and one of them on page 40 — if you count the back cover and introduction as part of the book and . . . why wouldn't you? So, the cover proves we're experts on travel because we were too busy traveling to check our cover for accuracy.

It also says on the cover that we've been on the *QEII*. *QEII* is an abbreviation for *Queen Elizabeth II*. It's a huge, fancy cruise ship. I guess everyone's supposed to know that, but only one of us did and we're *both* world travelers (that's why we're qualified to write this book). We've never been on the *QEII*. Furthermore, we *knew* we weren't going to ever be on the *QEII* when we okayed the mention of it on the cover. The *QEII* isn't even mentioned *once* (like Motel 6) in the book, except for the cover, once in the first Motel 6 paragraph, seven times in this paragraph (twice written out as *Queen Elizabeth II*, but that counts) and the closing. That just means we're liars and therefore *very* qualified to write a Penn & Teller book.

We hope you like it.

PENN JILLETTE and TELLER
On the Road — from Motel 6 to The Plaza
— but not on the QEII

PENN & TELLER'S
HOW TO PLAY IN TRAFFIC

THE ETERNAL CARD TRICK

SOME PEOPLE GET TO BE IMMORTAL, AND some don't.

My Aunt Tillie didn't. I was eight when she died, and I went with my parents to Delaware to clean out her farmhouse. All that was left was a pile of embroidered antimacassars, a pedal-pump pipe organ, and a chicken house. Tillie and all she had learned and thought in eighty-eight years were gone.

Even at the age of eight, I saw there was a fundamental difference between Aunt Tillie and Shakespeare. My parents had a set of Shakespeare's plays in the bookcase in their living room. I found I could pull out the yellowed, leather-bound volume of *Macbeth* and instantly murderers and fiends would come alive in my head. Shakespeare could still make me think and feel things, even though his body was a maggot snack almost four hundred years ago. Like a demon, I thought, he takes over the minds and bodies of living beings to prolong his own life. I envied him.

In high school I studied Latin. I figured if I learned the language of Caesar, Cicero, and Vergil — guys who have been immortal even longer than Shakespeare — I might catch on to their secret. Dr. Eichelberger, my Latin teacher, was fond of showing us ancient tombstone inscriptions. The best one was *Sum quod eris* which translates, "I am what you will be." At the end of his anonymous life, some old Roman found a way to have the last laugh, and his joke let him live forever.

I'm grown up now. I haven't left the world any classical orations, epic poems, or timeless tragedies. I haven't cured the common cold or discovered the magnetic monopole. I have no right to immortality. But thinking about the droll old fellow under the "I am what you will be" stone gave me an idea.

I've spent most of my adult life as half of Penn & Teller, a team of relatively honest tricksters. If we can bequeath to the world one lasting trick — as that Roman left us one still-piquant jibe — maybe we can finagle our way onto the roster of immortals, just as the smart-alecky Roman did.

I think we've found it. An eternal card trick. Buried in this book like a time capsule. Burning into the future like the flame on JFK's grave.

Picture this.

You are vacationing in Southern California and plan a day of sightseeing that includes visiting the graves of movie stars at the Forest Lawn Memorial Park in the Hollywood Hills. Over breakfast, you hand your vacation companion a deck of cards and have her/him pick one and — without looking at it — seal it in an envelope. You say, "I'll finish the trick later," and ask your comrade to bring the sealed envelope along on the day's excursion.

You commence sightseeing. When you arrive at Forest Lawn Memorial Park, you wander among the famous graves. You stand reverently beside Buster Keaton. You get your picture taken on Stan Laurel. Then suddenly you stop and stare, startled, at a grave marker.

"Look!" you exclaim, pointing to a dignified bronze memorial tablet on your right. "They must have shot each other doing that crazy bullet trick."

Here is what you're pointing at:

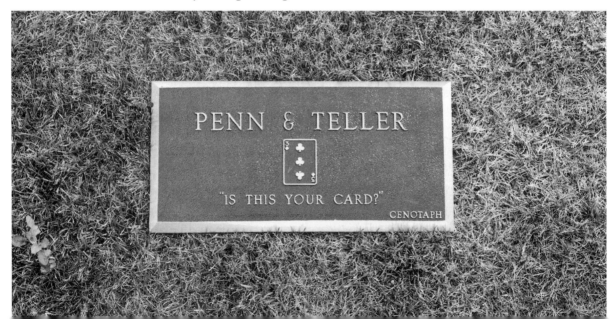

With a gasp, you "remember" the sealed envelope. You ask your friend to open it and look at the card. It matches the picture of the card on the monument.

From beyond the grave, Penn & Teller have given you the punch line to your trick.

Your friend passes out. You take snapshots.

That's a great trick. There's only one problem. You, reading this page today, might be stuck waiting twoscore years or so for us to croak before you get to enjoy our transcendental swindle. You might start *hoping* we have a bad accident, just so you can get to do your new trick. You might decide to help out.

That doesn't please us. We love life and have no desire to make you wish we were dead. So we cheated. We bought the farm now.

We purchased our piece of "permanent real estate" (as the plot-salesman called it) at Forest Lawn Memorial Park in the Hollywood Hills. We designed ourselves a "cenotaph" — that means a memorial marker that doesn't have to have a rotting corpse under it — they're usually used for people lost at sea but we've extended the meaning to include "and maybe they're not even dead yet." We have planted our cenotaph with quiet good taste and have drawn a map to help you find it without fumbling.

All you have to learn to do is make your friend pick the Three of Clubs.

Then go to the graveyard. Your punch line is waiting.

What you are about to learn is technically called a "card force." You are going to make your victim choose the Three of Clubs while being utterly convinced the choice was fair and random.

First, get a pack of cards. They always have them at hotel gift shops. Or maybe you want to splurge and pay ten bucks for one out of the mini-bar — that's up to you. Long before you start the trick, sneak the Three of Clubs out of the pack.

Now, locate an envelope. Most hotels give you a few in the little vinyl "Welcome!" folder that contains the room-service menu and commercials for the seaweed facial at the spa. Hide the Three of Clubs face down *under* the envelope. Have a pen nearby.

Hand your victim the pack of cards, and instruct, "Please shuffle these to your heart's content, then deal them facedown on the table until you feel an impulse to stop." Encourage her or him to keep dealing until absolutely satisfied with the stopping point.

While the shuffling and dealing take place, walk away, and open a couple of drawers, as if you are looking for supplies. "Find" the pen and the envelope — with the Three of Clubs *facedown* underneath.

Once the dealing is complete, return to your friend and hand him or her the pen. Immediately say, "What time is it, exactly?" For a moment, your friend will be occupied with the pen and the question, which will prevent any attention from going to the table as you *casually drop the envelope* (with the Three of Clubs under it) *on top of the cards that have just been dealt*, making the Three the top card of the pile on the table.

When your friend answers, immediately point to the envelope and say, "Write the date and exact time right here." Your friend does so. You continue, "Then take the last card you dealt, seal it inside without looking at it, and sign your name across the sealed flap." Your friend lifts up the envelope, and takes the top card off the stack (now, of course, your Three of Clubs), puts it into the envelope and seals it. As soon as you're sure the right card has gone into the envelope, step away again and stare out the window as if trying to avoid coming anywhere near the cards.

Don't rush any of this. Your friend has no reason to suspect anything. Nothing amazing seems to be happening yet. So be brazen. Look your chum calmly in the eye, ask your question, drop your envelope, and go right on with the directions. Later your friend will remember only that he/she shuffled the cards, picked one truly at random without you even touching them, and sealed the card in an envelope. In retrospect, this will make the trick a miracle.

Say, "Slip the sealed envelope into your wallet or someplace secure, and take it with you when we go out today. I'll finish the trick later." This is very important. If you do your dramatic grave-yard punch line and your audience replies, "How would I know if that's the right card? I left the envelope back at the hotel," you'll wish *you* were dead.

Be sure and take your camera along and immortalize your moment of triumph. And, incidentally, you might want to take a few slides or a videotape of the grave, so you can do the trick back home as the climax of your post-vacation slide show.

If you do your part and buy copies of this book for every teenager you know, and they do the same when they're adults, the Eternal Card Trick should take care of our immortality for at least a couple hundred years.

But we realize that no tombstone is really eternal. Someday JFK's flame will go out. In a thousand years somebody will pay off somebody on the zoning board and build a teleportation terminal where our graves used to be.

Then what will happen? With no grave to visit and no punch line for the card trick, will we vanish like Aunt Tillie? Maybe — and maybe not. We did one thing Tillie never did. We wrote this book.

The Latin writer Horace said in a poem, *Exegi monumentum aere perennius,* "I have raised a monument more lasting than bronze." He was talking about his poem. Romans bragged a lot, but in this case Horace was just stating a fact. Poetry, being digital, doesn't scratch or chip. That's the big advantage of literature over sculpture. Two millennia later, the glory of Rome lies in ruins, but Horace's little poem is as bright and egotistical as the day it was minted.

Now, we realize we're no Horace, nor are our words the flower of any Golden Age. On the other hand, I'm not depending on quality, as Horace did. Remember, for the first fourteen hundred years after he wrote his poems, they were reproduced *by hand*. Scribes don't waste time copying something unless they're convinced it's *really* important. Horace had to be great just to survive.

We don't have to be that great. Our first edition is 200,000 copies. The text is not just on paper, either; it's on negatives and plates and the hard drives of a dozen computers all over the country. It would pretty much take a nuclear holocaust to blow this book off the face of the planet. And if there's just one surviving copy . . . well, then, the whole cycle can begin again. Ironic, isn't it? In the long run, our words are more likely to endure than the Mona Lisa, no matter how carefully they control the humidity in the Louvre.

It would, however, be rude for us to neglect our probable, long-range audience. So:

Dear Reader of the Unimaginably Remote Future,

Thank you for taking the trouble to translate this book out of the inelegant idiom of twentieth-century American. We know how tough an ancient language can be.

We apologize that the punch line on our gravestones did not make it to your age. It was a fine trick — it really was. But we're guessing you folks probably don't play cards anymore anyway, and we don't imagine you waste much arable acreage on dead bodies.

If you still do tricks and people still die, feel free to adapt our idea to fit your own world. We'd be honored if we could provide a little inspiration to devious people in the future. If you don't want to go to the trouble, we understand. We'd be lazy, too, if our lives were disease-and-anguish-free, all the ills of the world having long since been banished by science and philosophy. But if that's the case, do us one small favor.

Read this, and know that long, long ago, when computers were the latest rage, when quantum physics seemed to hold all the answers, when outer space was unexplored and nations still quarreled over little patches of dirt — there lived two eccentric guys who did a few cool things.

Here's a map to help you find our cenotaph without bothering the folks at the front gate. Please remember that our grave *may* be funny (just now at least), but the graves around you are real, and real death can be very, very sad to the people left behind. So behave yourself and make your visit quiet and dignified. Besides, if you play it seriously, the trick's creepier.

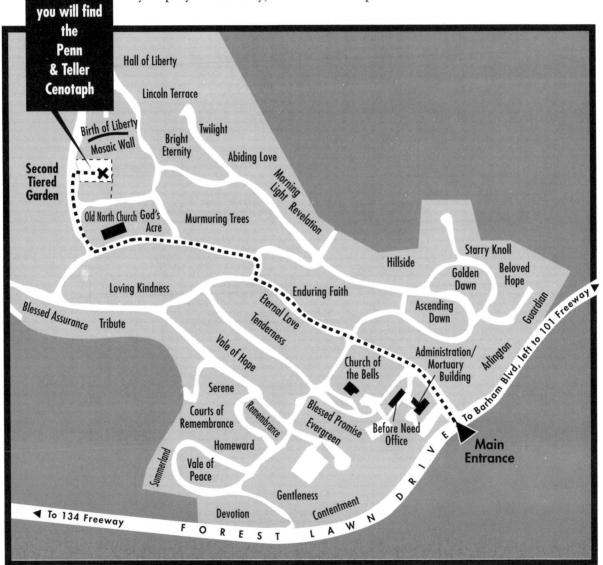

Here's where you will find the Penn & Teller Cenotaph

CARS: WIPERS AND HORNS
Tricks That Amuse & Confound
Penn & Teller, Respectively

If you're driving the car and Penn is the passenger and you want to make him laugh — sneeze all over the windshield. Don't cover your mouth, just let her rip (I don't mean any disrespect towards women by pronoun-sexing flying phlegm, it just sounded right, you know, kind of a "thar she blows" Moby thang). Let that 200-mile-an-hour nose wind blow free. Sneeze all over the windshield. As the snot hits the windshield, don't look at Penn, don't do anything, just reach down and turn on the windshield wipers for a couple beats. We're telling you — Penn'll have to leave the car horizontal — this gag kills him.

We need to thank Ken Klosterman for this next trick. (Ken Klosterman is the bread king of the greater Ohio area, a magician, a

Preparing to make Penn laugh

magic collector, and a great guy with a magic museum in an old mine shaft under his house. We have to thank Ken for so much, we're starting to resent it.)   Ken did this gag to Teller and fooled him. That's saying a lot and it's not saying much. When Teller's paying attention, no one ever fools him — when Teller's in his own world, the old now-it's-salt-now-it's-pepper gag can fool him in the material world. We don't know what universe he was groovin' in when Ken bamboozled him with this, but if it fooled him, it sure as shootin' would fool you. And if it'll fool you, dollars to doughnuts it'll fool the dreamers you hang with.

Teller was riding in Ken's fancy-ass BMW (bread kings have serious bread). Ken explained very seriously to Teller that the new Beamers (Ken doesn't talk like that, but let's pretend he does) have a "passenger horn" in case the passenger notices a hazard that the driver may have missed ("hazard" is such a great word.) He explained that the "passenger horn" was the ✳ button on the fancy-ass car phone.   (I tell you, bread kings make a couple-two-three dollars.) Ken demonstrated by reaching to the car phone near Teller's knee and pushing the ✳ button on the phone. The horn honked.

Of course the horn honked! *The horn honked because Ken pushed the horn button on the wheel at the same moment he hit the* ✳ *button!* But the Tellerfish took the hook, line, and sinker too far into the gullet for humane catch and release.

It's a cute, easy trick and if you don't have a fancy-ass BMW (which stands for Break My Windshield in our booklet), it's even better on a rental car. When you first slide behind the wheel of a totally unfamiliar automobile and head into the busy airport traffic of an unfamiliar city, keeping your mind on driving is just going to make you nervous. It's the perfect time to do a joke to get your mind off the road.

Start talking to your passenger about this new feature the federal government requires on new rental cars. (People will believe any ineffectual-zero-risk [redundant] nonsense [redundant again] from the federal government.)   Explain the federally mandated "passenger horn" to alert the driver to hazards (make sure you use that great word, "hazards") he or she may miss. Reach over to any button at all on the passenger side of the car. Glove box button? Cup holder?

Thumb on the horn button.

Preparing to hook the Teller-fish

Sure, what the hell do we care? Ken stung Teller with the ✳
button. Teller might have fallen for the phone's ♯, for christ's sake!

As you hit the "passenger horn" button with your right hand
(readers with automobiles built for use in Anguilla, Antigua, Aus-
tralia, Bahamas, Bangladesh, Barbados, Bhutan, Botswana, British
Virgin Islands, Brunei, Cayman Islands, Channel Islands, Christmas
Island, Cocos Islands, Cook Islands, Falkland Islands, Fiji, Granada,
Guyana, Hong Kong, India, Indonesia, Ireland, Isle of Man,

POSSIBLE HORN BUTTONS

Jamaica, Japan, Kenya, Kiribati, Lesotho, Macao, Malta, Mauritius, Montserrat, Mozambique, Namibia, Nauru, Nepal, New Zealand, Pakistan, Papua New Guinea, Pitcairn Island, St. Helena, St. Kitts, Nevis, St. Lucia, Singapore, Solomon Islands, Somalia, South Africa, Sri Lanka, Suriname, Swaziland, Tanzania, Thailand, Trinidad and Tobago, Turks and Caicos Islands, Uganda, United Kingdom, Virgin Islands (U.S.) and practical joking rural postmen, please reverse "left" and "right" in the previous and following phrases), you secretly push the real steering wheel horn button with your left hand.

Hey, it fooled Teller and that always makes Penn laugh.

THE
SSA ETHERIDGE,
A THURMAN,
EL GIBSON,
&
E DAVIDSON
TRICK

GEEKS. MAGIC IS FOR BOYS
ular. (Soon, as sexual equality spreads
e, we're hoping socially unskilled girls will
Professional magicians aren't babes. The
ut sexy stars. Magicians are either asexual
ple from the audience so they can flirt with
right. Some finally get enough money and
to act sexually attracted to them and that's
maybe Lance Burton does okay.
gicians that some people honestly find

1. Lance Burton

If you want to use magic to entice females, you'd better be doing card tricks in a women's correctional facility with a tux full of pardons. That's the deal for pros, but what about hobbyists? There are amateur magicians who are very attractive. Mel Gibson is a big magic fan and he ain't no geek. What about Mel? We don't want to be solipsistic. We don't want Mel to feel left out. Just because we're geeks doesn't mean that every person reading this book is a geek. No way.

The next trick is for people who have no trouble finding sexual partners. This is a trick you can do if you're beating sex partners off with a stick.

We've called this trick "The Melissa Etheridge, Uma Thurman, Mel Gibson, & Jaye Davidson Trick" because those are four different kinds of people that we're guessing don't have any trouble finding sex partners right to their taste. They're very attractive people in every way, and we know that at least Mel is into magic. And, if Uma doesn't find this trick to her liking, she can just let us know and we'll write some special material. We'd do it for Jaye and Melissa, too, of course; Uma was just an example.

It's very easy for us to write stuff like, "Wait until you're sitting next to someone that you want to freak out on an airplane." That's easy. But this next trick is way hypothetical. It's speculative fiction. Remember, we're geeks.

A TRICK
FOR THE *VERY*
SEXUALLY ATTRACTIVE

Did You Ever Have to Make Up Your Mind?

Some nights it's clear who you want to take back to your room, but most nights there are just too many choices. This is a trick for those occasional nights when you have it narrowed down to exactly two.

Look at your two potential sex partners and say:

"I find you both very attractive, but I consider sex to be an advanced form of communication. If all the nonverbal signals aren't working, sex isn't going to work. I have to find out if we can read each other. I have to find that out before we go any further. Here's my room key."

At this point, you dangle your room key (nowadays, mostly a credit card type thing) in front of both of them and then hand it to either one of them. (This is a travel book, so we're assuming that you're staying in an hotel. If you want to try it on home turf, any shiny, attractive object will do.)

"Here's my room key. It's where I'd like to have sex — if I feel there's the right kind of communication. I can't read your mind, I can only judge you by your actions. As a very famous geeky magician kinda said: if someone asks me to read his or her mind, I can't, but if someone punches me in the face, I have a pretty good idea what he or she is thinking. If he hadn't been such a geek, he might have pointed out that deciding to go to bed with someone gives them some idea what you're thinking as well. But magicians get hit more than they get asked to bed. Anyway, actions speak louder than words. I need to take control of the situation — you must listen to me carefully and do exactly what I ask. This is not necessarily the way it has to be in bed — this is just for this little test. If we're communicating well, if I can read you, I'll always know whether you are lying or telling the truth.

"I will turn my back and one of you two babes is to put my room key somewhere on your person. It doesn't make any difference which one of you holds the key, it has no bearing on who ends up with it after the test. And it doesn't matter where you put it as long as it's out of my sight and as close to one of your bodies as possible. So, one of you take it, and secure it on your person. I repeat, don't worry, the one without the key in this test has just as good a chance of ending up with the key."

You turn your back and let them fight over the key until one of them hides it on his or her body. You would probably guess that the one smiling the hardest has the key, but don't go by that — they could fool you. Use our trick. Continue with your patter:

"Now, there are three types of people in this world: those who tell the truth all the time no matter what, those who lie all the time no matter what, and those who do both. To see how good our communication is, we will deal only with the two extremes — those who lie all the time, and those who tell the truth all the time. I want you

both to decide in your own mind whether you want to always tell the truth, or whether you want to lie all the time. This is only a game: whatever you decide for this little test in no way reflects upon your true character. I won't judge you on which you pick. I'm not judging you, anyway. I'm judging us *on the overall test."*

Give them a moment to think and continue:

"Do you have it in your mind . . . please don't answer because if you have chosen to be a liar you would have to say no, and that could keep us here forever and I'm eager to get up to the room.

"For this test it's imperative that you each know what the other has chosen — liar or honest person. This is the only time the liar will be allowed to tell the truth. I will turn my back, and you will let the other person know whether you've decided to lie or tell the truth. I don't want to overhear you, so please whisper very quietly in each other's ear while my back is turned. Please make sure I don't hear. To make it easier to keep the information from me, I'll cover my ears and sing to myself while you exchange information. Okay, get ready to whisper."

Turn your back, cover your ears, and sing to yourself "Do Ya Think I'm Sexy?" or anything by Nine Inch Nails. Feel free to dance a little. When they've had time for a bit of whispering, turn back around to face them again.

"Let's recap: one of you has my room key hidden on your body. No way I could know who has it. On top of that you both freely chose whether you would always lie or always tell the truth. No way for me to know what you chose. Only the two of you know what you chose to be, and only you two know what the other person chose to be.

"There are numerous choices you could have made. You [touch one of them in some very sexy way — you know better than I do] could have chosen to tell the truth and you [touch the other] could have chosen to be a liar, or it could be the other way around. Then again, you could have both chosen to be the same thing, you could

both be telling the truth or you could both be flirting with lying. Asking what you have chosen would not tell me anything, because if I ask you if you are telling the truth and you are, you will say yes; but if you're not telling the truth, you will also say yes. So, there is no way for me to know who is telling me the truth and who isn't. Yet, I may be able to tell by your body, by your eyes, by the way you move, by the way you speak. If I can do that, we're really communicating."

I would suggest giving them both deep, sexy, thoughtful looks at this point, but what the hell do I know — you're the one that can get laid.

Turn to the first person:

"Remember, if you chose to be honest, tell the truth. If you chose to lie, you have to lie to me now. Answer only yes or no! Just 'yes' or 'no.' Do you have my room key in your possession?"

Turn to the second person and ask the same question using the exact same lines.

While you're asking these questions, work it. Take this time to really check out your potential sex partners. Look them up and down. Violate them with your eyes.

(Legal note: do not try this trick in the workplace.)

"Wow, that was pretty easy. I can read you both like a book. Wow, vibe city." (I don't think a really sexy person would say "vibe city," so say something different, something that a sexy person would say.)

"I know who has my room key, but I want to ask one more question."

Turn to the first person. *"Remember, if you're honest — tell the truth. If you're a liar — you have to lie again. Only yes or no! Did you both decide to be the same type of person?"*

While they're answering, check them out. Check out the eyes, the lips, check all the parts you care about and a few you like to pretend to care about.

Turn to the second person and ask the same question with the same checking out.

"I now know who has my room key, and I know exactly what type of person you decided to be. You see, I saw one of those perfect brown eyes blink for a little too long when you told me you did not have my room key — you do have it. You were lying to me, you little scamp. You did that exact same thing with your perfect eyes when I asked you if y'all decided to be the same kind of person. You said yes, but those eyes told me that our other new friend was telling the truth, when denying having my room key."

Obviously, you make this section fit the situation on the lying or truth telling and what body part gave it away. I'm fond of mentioning a "heaving bosom" here and there, but what do I know? You continue by talking to the second person:

"You were telling the truth when you said you did not have my room key and when you said you both were not the same kind of person. But I wanted to check it. You bit that full bottom lip and looked me straight in the eye — very sexy. I knew you were telling the truth."

Address the first potential play partner again:

"Did you choose, just for this game, to be a liar? Please tell the truth now — this game is over."

You are right. Turn to the second person.

"And you, my sweet [jesus, when we try to write sexy, we sound like Pepé LePew], *did you choose to try honest for a while?"*

You're right, of course. You continue:

"Wow, I learned a lot about both of you. There's a lot of communication here. A lot of communication."

You turn to the person with the key.

"May I have my room key please?"

It's removed from its hiding place (let's hope this involves reaching into a sexy place) and you were right. You dangle the key, seductively (you know how to do that), in front of both of them.

"Hmm. I'm good at this, but it's never been that easy before. The communication among us is astonishing. I can tell every little thought that goes through your very attractive heads. I'm flabbergasted. I was hoping to use this little test to judge and choose, but . . . I can't. I think the communication is so perfect, all three of us should go up to my room right now and find out how perfect the communication can be. Come on."

(Of course, you could say that you figured it all from one person and lose the other, but who on Earth would do that? Huh? Well, I don't know, maybe sexy people are crazy.)

How do you do it? I have no idea, I guess it's genetic, you know, looks and charm and . . . oh, sorry, how is *the trick* done? Oh, that. The trick is very easy. When you ask the first question, *"Do you have the room key?"* you remember the first reply. It will *not* tell you who has the room key *yet*. It will not tell you anything until you find out, with the second question, who's telling the truth and who's lying. Asking the room key question first is misdirection. You need to remember the answer, but don't worry about it, all the real work is in the second question. The second question — "Did you both choose to be the same type of person?"— asked to either one, tells what the *other* person is.

If one says "no," the *other* person is a liar; if one says "yes" the *other* person is telling the truth. That's why you need to ask both people the question, so you'll know what both people decided. It's a little hard to believe, that's why it's a good trick, but it works just like that. Let's lay it out for you.

If they're both honest and you ask one if they're both the same, you get a "yes" and you know the other is honest. If the one you're asking is a liar and you ask if they're both the same and you get a "yes," you know that the other is honest. So, no matter whether the person you're talking to is honest or lying, if you get a "yes," the *other* is honest. Neat, huh?

Okay, how about when the person you're *not* asking has chosen to be a *liar*? Well, if they're both lying then the answer to "are you both the same?" will be "no" (because they *are* the same, get it?) so the "no" tells you the other is a liar. And if the one you're asking has chosen honesty, then the answer to "are you both the same?" is "no" and the other is a liar.

If you need more explanation — read it again. Or, if that's too much work, just take our word for it (often a bad idea): If one person says "yes" the *other* is honest and if that person says "no" the *other* is a liar. Each person tells you what the other person is and it's pretty easy to remember that "yes" means honest and "no" means liar. I guess you could try laying it out graphically, but the grid we originally created for the book confused the copy editor, and he was reading more carefully than you. Just do the trick a few times and you'll get it.

Once you know who is lying and who is telling the truth, you know who has the room key. Everything else is just flirting and lying (very similar skills, at least for us).

THINK GORILLA

WHENEVER WE TRAVEL, WE LOOK FOR FAIRS: blazing lights, blasting music, gluttony, lust, morbid curiosity — show business in all its profit-making splendor, bare-naked with no "this-is-Art-not-commerce" doubletalk to confuse you.

We were running our show on Broadway one summer, and it was our night off, a Monday. We heard there was a fair just across the Hudson River at the Meadowlands stadium fairground in New Jersey. We rented a car and drove out, calculating our arrival to coincide with sunset, when a fair gets sexy.

It was a hot, humid July evening, perfect for T-shirt, shorts, and sneakers. Myself, I wore a white Italian sport coat with a window-pane check, ivory cotton trousers, and two-tone wing tip shoes. I like looking snappy when I go to a fair.

We paid three bucks to park, five for tickets, then headed through the turnstile, and down the midway, straight for the Human Oddities tent. The proprietors, Ward and Chris, are friends of ours. They welcomed us like brothers and let us in for free. We breezed by the mummies and the pickled punks (mutant fetuses in formaldehyde), and watched the fat man do his cool dance, and our pal the "blockhead" drive spikes into his sinuses. After we'd seen one cycle of the show, the boss took us back into his private trailer, served colas, told stories, and gave us a stack of free ride passes. Show folk know how to treat their own.

Eventually we said goodbye to our friends and moved on down the midway. I was hoping to spot a men's room, but before I did, we encountered the Girl-to-Gorilla attraction. I walked right up and paid the one-dollar admission for myself *and* my partner. I'm a big spender when I'm wearing two-tone shoes.

But what's that you say? You've never seen a Girl-to-Gorilla?
Well, then, sit back and let me tell you all about it.

On a platform outside the tent a barefoot, bored young woman in a leopard-spot bikini stands in a cage. A brittle loudspeaker tells the crowd that she is Zamora, the beautiful victim of a cruel medical experiment. "You will see the clothing fall away from her breasts and her skin sprout stiff black fur." Now, that's a show you don't want to miss.

"Everyone gets in on a child's one-dollar ticket. One dollar, this show and this show only," says the recording. "Show starting in just one minute." The bikinied woman puts on her slippers, leaves the cage, and enters the tent. You hesitate. It has to be a hoax, you think. Then you see others going in, and you decide: Hey, what's to lose? It's only a buck.

The inside of the Girl-to-Gorilla show is austere. The stage is the rear end of a truck backed into a tent. The curtain is a square of canvas hanging on a wire. There are no seats; all performances are S.R.O.

After five or ten minutes, when the tent is more or less full and before the crowd gets rowdy, a sunburnt, rawboned guy slides in through the back, lowers the lights, and flips on a recording.

The grating voice on the tape tells you that Zamora's father was a biochemist in need of a subject for his experiments in gene-splicing. He injected the tender girl with a serum he hoped would strengthen her resistance to disease. Instead it rearranged her genetic code and turned her into a monster. It is not a pretty story.

The sunburnt guy yanks away the canvas curtain. Behind a set of bars, deep in the shadows of the truck stands Zamora, sullenly leaning against a corner.

She is clearly the same living, breathing, bored human being you saw on the platform outside.

"Think gorilla. Think gorilla," the recording says. "Gorilla, gorilla, gorillagorillagorillagorilla," and Zamora looks pained.

"Gorillagorillagorillagorillagorilla!"

And she begins to change.

Slowly, her smooth skin fades and in its place you see stiff black fur. Her eyes gleam from sockets that grow deeper and deeper. It's like a cinematic lap-dissolve, but with no movie screen between you and the miracle. Eventually, the only hint of the woman Zamora once was is a transparent flicker of her leopard-skin brassiere on the massive hairy chest; then the bra fades, too. Zamora is all ape.

Now, of course *you* don't believe you're actually watching a woman descending the evolutionary ladder. You know it's an optical illusion of some kind. You may even know how it works.

But on a hot night in a dim carny tent, a girl-turned-gorilla — even if she's behind bars, even if she's not a real gorilla — makes you very attentive, the way you get attentive when they keep you too long at the top of the Ferris wheel and you hear the gondolas creak.

And then . . . the ape begins to move. Towards you.

"Wait a minute. What's wrong?" says the voice on the tape. The gorilla is now slamming against the steel walls of the truck, and advancing towards the bars at the mouth of the cell. "Get back! Zamora, back! Back!" But Zamora doesn't listen. She rattles the bars. "Back, Zamora, back!" But it's too late.

Ape-Zamora heaves her weight at the iron gate of her cell, the hinges give way, and the bars crash to the floor with a deafening clang (a metal plate in the stage makes the sound just right). Strobe lights flash. Alarm bells and ambulance sirens shriek. Some people scream, others laugh, but everybody scurries for the exit flap — conveniently held open by the rawboned guy, saying, "This way out, folks."

As the tent closes, if you look back, you can just spot the rogue primate calmly re-entering her den.

That was the show we saw. We had seen it before, many times, with other Zamoras in other tents on other fairgrounds. At its best, Girl-to-Gorilla is an inspiration, a reminder of how potent a magic trick can be. At its worst, it still beats Andrew Lloyd Webber.

Back on the midway, I remembered I needed that men's room. Glancing down the alley beside the Girl-to-Gorilla tent, I could just make out the gleam of a portable toilet. I slipped into the darkness, away from the light and noise of the midway.

I walked between the trucks and tents, past a small silver trailer with scalloped chiffon curtains, and was just stepping into the dirty white booth, when I heard a voice yell, "Hey!"

I pretended not to hear and closed the door behind me. I was backstage uninvited, and it's always easier to be forgiven than to get permission.

When I emerged from the toilet, I found myself facing the back of a truck. The vinyl flap was pulled aside, and a large, shirtless, sweaty young man, lying on his side, was watching me.

"Hey. C'm'ere." He spoke with a soft Caribbean accent. "Zamora tells me you're on cable TV sometimes."

"Uh, sure. I mean I have been."

"Who are you?" he asked. I told him and we shook hands. "How do you do," he said. "I'm the gorilla."

His name was Dana and he was from Virginia where his dad is a baker. Suddenly the door of the trailer with scalloped curtains popped open and Zamora appeared wearing a T-shirt over her leopard-skin bikini. "See?" she said to Dana, "It *was* them at the show."

She turned to me. "What are *you* doing *here*?" she said, as if she suspected my chauffeur had mistakenly dropped me at the fair instead of the Waldorf-Astoria.

"Um, I like the rides and the food and the shows."

Zamora and Dana looked at each other.

"Really," I said, "you guys do a great show. It looks so great when the bra fades out over the gorilla's chest."

"Really?"

Now, I wasn't being gracious. Girl-to-Gorilla is perfect theatre, as visceral as Shakespeare, as ironic as Brecht, and powerful enough to blast the audience right out of the tent. All that and cheaper than a corn dog.

But an alley by the crapper didn't seem the right place for a dissertation on the consanguinity of the arts. Besides, doubtful Zamora and sweaty Dana had five more shows to do that evening. So we just smiled and shook hands and went our separate ways, they to their cage, I to the Tilt-a-Whirl.

I was happy. I had impressed a Girl, and talked to a Gorilla. The night was young. And I had a pocket full of free ride passes.

RAINDROPS ON ROSES, WHISKERS ON KITTENS, TOM, A CLOWN NOSE . . . AND MAYBE A FREE UPGRADE

TOM MULLICA IS A FUNNY MAN. A VERY FUNNY man. Tom Mullica is also a very good magician and a man you don't want to play pool against for money. Tom Mullica is a kind, gentle man, who sincerely wants everyone on our finely evolved Earth to be a little happier. It is so hard not to hold that against him. You may have seen Tom on TV with a zillion cigarettes in his mouth.

Tom Mullica — He's a funny guy.

Tom, like most show folk, spends a lot of time traveling. He plays clubs all over the world, so he knows his way around a fuselage. He carries a gimmick with him that *often* gets him upgrades on airplanes. It also gets him better service in restaurants, better parking spaces, applause on public transportation, and saves him from being reprimanded when he deserves it. It's not a scam, it's not a rip-off. You don't have to lie and there are no suckers. (It's hard to believe we just typed that last sentence. We feel dirty.) Tom's brilliant idea just makes people happier. It makes the world a better place. Here's Tom's Nobel Prize quality idea: Tom carries a clown nose in his right-hand jacket pocket.

That's really stupid, right? We mean, big deal, so he carries a clown nose. So what? Well, sew buttons on Easter bunnies. (Sorry, we were caught up in that sweetness and light thing.) We'll tell you so what. He also carries his state and national identification cards in the same pocket. He keeps his driver's license and passport in the pocket with his clown nose. So what? Well, stay with us. He's altered his identification with a small piece of foam and some rubber cement. His identification looks like this:

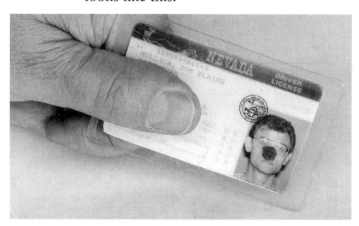

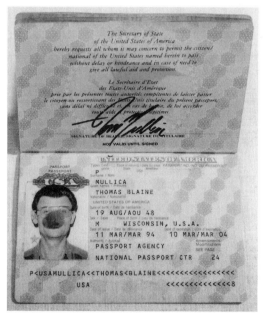

With these official papers and clown nose Tom does a lot more for the world than that self-serving glory-hogging Mother Teresa ever did.

When asked for I.D. at the gate or ticket counter of an airline, Penn gets crazy. He either sulks or rants against the pig power structure and the statism and zero-risk thinking that's encroaching on our freedom. When Tom sees an identity check approaching, Tom gets happy. When the put-upon bureaucrat, sad and weakened from trying to deal politely with the misplaced anger of misguided uptight fools like Penn, asks for Tom's I.D., Tom just smiles. When he reaches into his right-hand jacket pocket to get his I.D., he also cops the clown nose. There's no palming involved, he just holds the clown nose in the palm of his hand while holding his passport between his index finger and thumb (don't worry about it, it's the way *you* hold your passport or license except, up until now, you haven't also had a clown nose in your hand). He hands the clerk his passport. They aren't looking for a red nose in his hand.

The soon-to-be-laughing bureaucrat looks down at the passport and sees the mixed media passport art with the little pea-sized foam nose over the picture of Tom's nose. This is a little funny. This low man or woman on the airline totem pole smiles gently and looks up. Tom, during this giggling misdirection, has slipped the full-sized clown nose over his full-sized nose. How funny is this? How good an idea is this?

This is how good an idea it is:

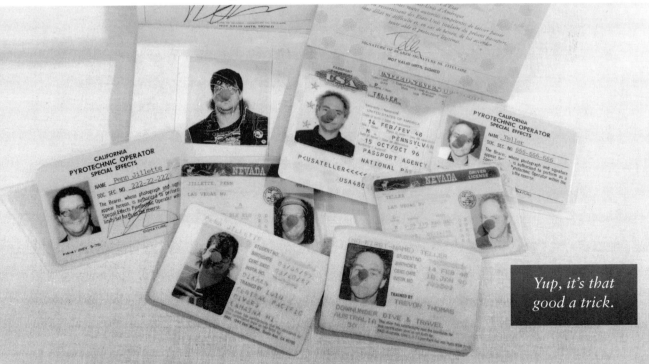

Yup, it's that good a trick.

 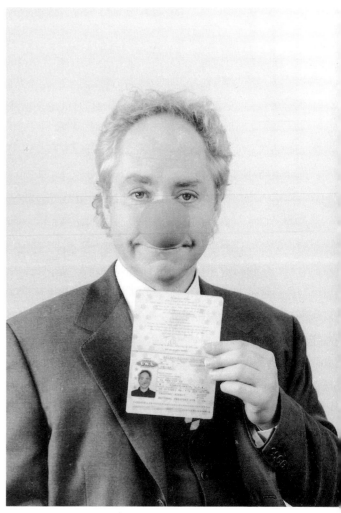

Imagine the joy.

One of the pictures above should have been a joke. It should have been a change-up. Maybe a different angle with a clerk punching Penn or at least looking disgusted, or way unamused, or something. That would have been a P&T style joke — but, we didn't do it. We didn't do it, because those things don't happen with this gag. This trick makes *everyone* happy. *Everyone* laughs. You can't lose. Tom says they *often* upgrade him to first class just because they want to do something for him after that white-light-white-heat shot of pure joy. Tom's been doing this gag forever. And he does it everywhere.

Oh, ye of little faith, now you're thinking, "Not to peace officers! Not while waiting for a speeding ticket or after being caught trying to pull off a hit-and-run!" You, sir, or madam, are wrong. Tom does it everywhere. Police like to laugh, too. Tom has gotten out of speeding tickets. Who knows? We might find out that Tom was D.B. Cooper — he just gave them his clown nose I.D. and strolled with the cash.

Of course the clown nose is best when set up with the I.D. but Tom is always ready to whip it out. If a little kid is crying on the bus — Tom slips on the nose, the kid stops screaming, and Tom gets applause. If he accidentally (so he says) cuts off someone in traffic or steals a parking space — Tom puts on the nose and when the stranger looks over to scream at Tom, and make whatever hand gestures are appropriate to the culture — the evil just disappears. (Tom thinks it's because they're so full of joy. It could also be that they don't want to mess with someone who's mentally ill.)

This is a fake picture.

At Tom's wedding, when his life mate turned around to look during "if anyone sees a reason for these two, blah, blah, blah," the entire crowd was wearing clown noses. Tom had handed them out before the ceremony and gave them a cue.

"Okay, this is going too far."

We're converts. We've started doing it. Whether you're cute like Teller or big and scary like Penn, with a clown nose, you're funny. Penn now looks forward to the fascist security checks that are destroying the very idea of our free country.

I guess we should tell ya how to do it, huh? That's part of the book. We have to explain 'em. How stupid do we have to pretend you are? Okay. Glue a little round piece of red foam rubber to your I.D. with rubber cement. Get a clown nose at a magic or joke shop. If you don't have a clown nose shop (usually spelled "shoppe") in your town, you can do what Tom does and what we did: You can make a clown nose.

. . . Okay, we'll tell you how. Get a red (color is important, don't mess with an icon) sponge ball (of course the *only* place we've ever seen that sells sponge balls is a magic store, so . . . we're sorry, but you're going to have to go to a magic store) and cut a slit in it with a razor blade (if you're old enough to read, you should know how big your nose is). Put your gimmicked I.D. and the clown nose in an easily accessible pocket and get ready to be bumped to first class.

Tom explains that people are uptight, irritable, on edge, and redundant when traveling and the clown nose really helps break the tension. After a long talk about the joy he had brought into the world, Tom added, "Sometimes, if I'm really irritated and pissed off myself, I don't take the nose out."

We're glad he said that; he was starting to make us sick.

OUR FOURTH AMENDMENT'S LITTLE HELPER

THIS ISN'T A TRICK, A GAG, OR A STORY. It's a tool, a tool to help protect your privacy. I have often said, when I'm trying to say something grandiose, that the next big issue facing our nation (when you're trying to say something grandiose, "the next big issue facing our nation" is a damn fine way to start) is privacy. I argue for legal, non-government, private encryption software for computers, phones, and faxes, with no back door for the government. Wiretaps don't catch bad guys; bad guys being stupid catches bad guys.

The qualities of bad and stupid go together like, well, like Penn & Teller, for christ's sake. Show me something bad, and I'll show you something stupid. C'mon, show me, we'll have a blast. Smart things are hardly ever bad, and bad things are never smart. The smart bad guy is a literary device invented to give fictitious smart good guys someone to vanquish with a tad more suspense.

If the good guys in the F.B.I. (which is most of them) are trying to catch the head bad guy of a mob, they catch him because the bad guy is too stinkin' stupid to run an honest dry cleaning business in the neighborhood. (I'm not saying that dry cleaners are stupid, I could have picked any business, but dry cleaners struck me funny. Funny doesn't *necessarily* mean stupid — look at Gilbert Gottfried. Gil doesn't illustrate my point, but he sure is funny-looking.) The bad guy's high school classmates that were smart enough to work for a living are now working for a living. It's the dumb ones that chose the bad guy biz. It's a place where an immoral fool can get ahead for a while. Oh, sure, I guess there have been *some* smart bad people. Nixon seemed like kind of a smart bad person, but really he was more of a smart crazy person. Real, no kidding crazy *always* walks hand in hand with bad like, well, just like, well, Penn & Teller don't ever walk hand in hand, but you get the idea.

Even if you postulate a smart bad guy (we're using "guy" here to mean both sexes, like we always do, but if you haven't caught up to that usage, it's fine to picture a man here — only 6% of humans in prison are women and most of them are in for victimless crimes), a bad guy smart enough that the good guys couldn't get a thing on him without wiretaps, that smart person would be smart enough to foil the wiretap. He would talk on the phone in a verbal code or something. I don't know what that "something" would be. I'm smart enough to not be a bad guy but not smart enough to make up stuff that a theoretical smart bad guy could do to get around smart good guys. Wiretaps wouldn't work on smart people, and you can catch the damn, dumb, bad people other ways. We don't need no stinkin' wiretaps.

Benjamin Franklin didn't say, "He who would sacrifice liberty for safety deserves neither," but he said something very close to that, that a good friend of mine has been misquoting for years. I don't care if Ben Franklin said it, or just my friend Colin Summers said it — it's true. Every time something really bad happens, people cry out for safety, and the government answers by taking rights away from good people. We have no proof that the bad, stupid, crazy people who have planted bombs in the past few years used the phone much for their stupid bad crimes, let alone logged on the Internet. Yet when those kinds of bad things happen nowadays, the government tries to do bad stupid things to phones and the Net. The phones and the Internet are just good smart things, and the government should leave them alone. You have to watch the government all the time on everything. Thomas Jefferson didn't say that, but he said something very close to that.

Privacy is an important issue. But *our* privacy, our individual privacy, *your* personal privacy and *my* personal privacy, are not in any real danger. Not because a zillion people couldn't tap our phones, bug our personal conversations, and read all our love letters with trivial technology, but because not one of those zillion people cares. It's a little sad. If you or I go on a beach, take all our clothes off, and dance around, no one is going to take pictures and sell them to *Playboy*. We're just going to be told to put our clothes on and be reprimanded for scaring the children. Now, when I use the word "we" above, I'm assuming that Uma Thurman is not reading this book. If Ms. Thurman *is* reading this book, well, Uma, call our office and they'll give you my home number — I have grandiose ideas to discuss with you.

So, no one cares — and that protects your personal privacy. At least most of the time no one cares. I'm not making the argument that if we're doing nothing wrong, then we shouldn't be afraid of the government monitoring us. That's a stupid, bad argument. We should always be afraid of any government monitoring us. The fact that no one cares what we're talking about is an argument for keeping it that way. We don't want the government to be able to care. Any power you give the government, the government will try to abuse. George Washington almost said that.

There are a few places where us regular guys (and I do mean both sexes here — we like to pretend that our books are read by both sexes) — regular guys like us (yeah, sure) do have to worry about our privacy. We do have to worry about strangers reading over our shoulders. It's irritating enough when we're reading a newspaper or a work of fiction (a lesser person would make a cynical joke here about them being one and the same). But when you're typing on your laptop, and someone is reading what you're typing "over your shoulder," it must be stopped.

I'm writing this on an airplane and there's a man sitting next to me, and his beady, bored, nervous, infrequent flyer eyes keep wandering over to this screen. It's hard enough to type on this little keyboard on this stupid little tray table, without having to turn the computer almost sideways to make the LCD go psychedelic from his angle. With me typing straight in my seat, he can just read whenever he feels like it. It makes it hard for me to think. It makes it hard to work on a rough draft. I edit my writing, I really do, honest, no kidding. (As an example, I took out an "I swear on my mother's eyes" from the end of that last sentence. That's proof that I edit.) I don't want this guy next to me going away saying, "Jeez, I can't believe he's doing that awful Gallagher joke up there in the second 'graph." (See, I cut that joke, too. What more proof of editing do you need?) I want *everyone* to read this when I'm done with it, but I don't want *anyone* to read it before I'm done with it, before I cut out some of the bad stupid jokes.

So here's the tool I use and you can use it, too. Type the e-mail on the next page into your computer (change the sex or the war to make it fit your look) and keep it in a file in your root directory. If you feel someone reading over your shoulder, just pull up the fake letter and let it sit there for a while. Pretend to work on it a little. There's a very good chance the snoop will stop reading over your shoulder.

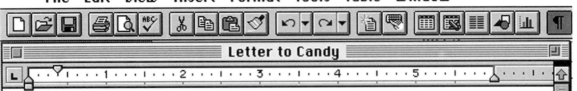

Letter to Candy

Candy Honey,

I feel like I'm living in the future. Being out of society nine and a half years makes you appreciate the freedom in the modern world. I love flying, it's so great to be soaring free in the air after all those months in the joint. Freebird, baby. I am now a free bird.

You would have been proud. I was good and didn't violate my parole when airport security took away my buck knife and colors. It wouldn't have bothered me at all except the buck knife was a freedom present from the motorcycle club. I don't need a knife to protect my privacy — I still have my Green Beret training. I remember once in 'Nam I tore out that man's heart with my bare hands and showed it to him before he was dead. He was a friend, and I didn't really want to kill him, but it made me crazy that he was looking at the pictures I was scratching in the dirt with a stick. Those pictures weren't for him. Yeah, he saw them, but not for long.

It scares me, honey, but I think I would do the same thing again if the situation came up. I would hate to go back to seeing you only through that cold glass wall — but I can't stand busybodies, prying eyes, nosey people. Why can't people keep to themselves?

You say the information on this computer is safe and no one will read over my shoulder. I hope you're right because I don't want to kill again. I will if I have to, but I don't want to go back to prison. If another offense means I get the chair — so be it. What I write is for you and me, and you and me alone. ¶

For Your Eyes Only,

Johnny Death

AT LAST: A USE FOR
THAT GIDEON BIBLE

GIDEON WAS AN ANCIENT HEBREW WHO rid Israel of a tribe of poachers called the Midianites. Gid's strategy was original. He armed three hundred warriors with lamps, pitchers, and trumpets. In the middle of the night they surrounded their enemy's camp and started blasting away on their horns. Having got the sleepy Midianites' attention, the attackers smashed their pitchers, brandished their lamps, and screamed, "The Sword of the Lord, and of Gideon!" The Midianites took one look at the raving, trumpet-playing, lamp-waving, pitcher-smashing Hebrews, then pulled up their stakes and ran away.

The modern Gideons International organization commemorates Gideon's sneak attack by sneaking bibles into other people's dresser drawers. The group's been around since the 1890s and claims they've distributed over 500,000,000 bibles to travelers all over the world. We're sorry they're not spelling fanatics instead of religious nuts. Imagine how handy it would be to find a dictionary in your night table, "Placed by The Doctor Johnsons."

But since you're stuck with a bible in your room, you might as well get some fun out of it. Now please understand: in the following trick it may *look* as if we're instructing you to mutilate your guest-room bible. Gosh, no. We'd never suggest that, because it's wrong to damage other people's property and because the Gideons might try to sue *us* for *your* vandalism.

So when we write about using the "Gideon bible" in your room, we are not talking about the real Gideon bible. We mean the *special* bible you went out and bought for this trick. It should look *exactly* like a Gideon bible and you should always carry it in your luggage. *Capisce?*

THE GIDEON BIBLE CARD TRICK

This is a card trick that looks like a satanic ritual. But unlike satanic rituals, it *works*.

It uses cards, a bible, and an iron. Middle-grade hotels and better generally hang an iron in your closet, but even a Motel 6 will provide one on request.

You take out your iron and let it heat up. Meanwhile, your friend shuffles a pack of cards and picks one while you are on the far side of the room. Now you bring out your Gideon bible.

You turn to Revelation, chapter 17, and tell your friend to read aloud verse 5, which is all about abominations, and sounds for all the world like an invitation to hell. You have your friend place one hand on the back of the chosen card, while with the other hand she/he *irons* the page of Revelation.

Slowly, brownish bloodstains appear on three isolated words of the text:

CHAPTER 17

And there came one of the seven angels which had the seven vials, and talked with me, saying unto me, Come hither; I will shew unto thee the judgment of the great whore that sitteth upon many waters:

2 With whom the kings of the earth have committed fornication, and the inhabitants of the earth have been made drunk with the wine of her fornication.

3 So he carried me away in the spirit into the wilderness: and I saw a woman sit upon a scarlet coloured beast, full of names of blasphemy, having seven heads and **ten** horns.

4 And the woman was arrayed in purple and scarlet colour, and decked with gold and precious stones and pearls having a golden cup in her hand full of abominations and filthiness **of** her fornication:

5 And upon her forehead was a name, written, MYSTERY, BABYLON THE GREAT THE MOTHER

8 The beast that thou sawest was

11 And the beast that was, and is not, even he is the eighth, and is of the seven, and goeth into perdition.

12 And the ten horns which thou sawest are ten kings, which have received no kingdom as yet, but receive power as kings one hour with the beast.

13 These have one mind, and shall give their power and strength unto the beast.

14 These shall make war with the Lamb, and the Lamb shall overcome them: for he is Lord of lords, and King of kings: and they that are with him are called, and chosen, and faithful.

15 And he saith unto me, The waters which thou sawest, where the whore sitteth, are peoples, and multitudes, and nations, and tongues.

16 And the ten horns which thou sawest upon the beast, these shall hate the whore, and shall make her desolate and naked, and shall eat her flesh and burn her with fire.

17 For God hath put in their **hearts** to fulfill his will, and to agree, and give their kingdom unto the beast, until the words of God shall be fulfilled.

How's that for a divine revelation?

DEVIL'S WORK?

No, not quite. All you need is lemon juice and a little sleight-of-bible.

1. Order a cup of tea with lemon from Room Service. Drink the tea and save the lemon. Then, when you can get a few minutes alone with your Gideon bible, open to Revelation (the last book of the bible), chapter 17.

Put a facial tissue behind the page you are gimmicking. Squeeze out some lemon juice into a saucer and use a cotton swab or a pencil eraser to drop a tiny droplet of juice right on the word "ten" in verse 3, the word "of" in verse 4, and the word "hearts" in verse 17. Let it soak in for two to three minutes. Then blot off the excess moisture with another tissue, and let the page dry. When it is dry, remove the tissue and close the bible.

2. Get a deck of cards. Hotel gift shops and even mini-bars generally have them, but if you've read enough of our books, you probably already carry a deck in your luggage, right beside your personal pseudo-Gideon bible. Remove the Ten of Hearts from the deck and stick it in your bible at Revelation, chapter 17. Put the bible in a dresser drawer.

3. Make sure the iron is handy and in working order.

4. While you are chatting with your friend, draw the shades and unplug the phone. Make it look like you're planning to do something very private, and possibly wicked. Strip naked (but of course we'd recommend that for enhancing any trick). Take out the iron and set it to "Permanent Press" (you'll find it just below "Wool").

5. Hunt around and "find" the bible. Pick it up and look through it musingly, being careful not to expose the hidden Ten of Hearts. Say, "You may not know it, but Saint John got his reputation as the Divine by doing card tricks. He left all his secrets coded in the last book of the bible. That's why it's called 'Revelation.' Here, I'll show you."

6. Bring out the deck of cards and ask your friend to shuffle them, then start dealing them one at a time — facedown — onto the desk (if there's no desk, do this on the floor). After eight or ten cards have been dealt, say, "Keep dealing. Then, whenever you like, stop. Tell me when you have stopped."

7. While your friend is dealing, turn your back. Open the bible to Revelation, chapter 17. Leave the book open, but slip the Ten of Hearts — facedown — underneath the book. (You're about to do the same force you use in The Eternal Card Trick, page 3.)

8. When your friend has stopped dealing, turn around with the open bible. Be careful not to let your friend see the Ten of Hearts hidden under the book. Plunk the book (and the hidden card) down right on top of the stack of cards your friend has just dealt. This adds your Ten of Hearts to the top of the stack.

9. Simultaneously point to verse 5 (the one printed mostly in capital letters) and tell your friend to read it aloud:

That should hold your friend's attention, eh? There's nothing like Harlots to make your friend forget you ever came near the stack of cards.

10. Now it's time for a little double-talk to introduce the iron. Tell your friend, "Look at the parallel column on the right-hand side of the page. That's where Saint John the Divine always puts the instructions for the trick. I think it's verse 16. Read the last phrase in the verse."

16 "And the ten horns which you saw on the beast, these will hate the harlot, make her desolate and naked, eat her flesh and burn her with fire.

Your friend reads out, "burn her with fire."

11. That's your cue to bring on the iron. Have your friend move the bible to an open spot on the table. Now ask your friend to place one hand on the stack of cards while he/she takes the iron in the other hand and *irons* the page of the bible.

WARNING: IRONS ARE HOT. IF YOU AND/OR YOUR FRIEND ARE TOO HAM-HANDED OR LAME-BRAINED TO HANDLE AN IRON WITHOUT BURN-ING YOURSELF, TRY ANOTHER TRICK.

12. Get your ironing friend to chant with you, "Mystery, Babylon the Great, the Mother of Harlots and abominations of the earth." Meanwhile the magic of chemistry is at work and the heat acts on the vitamin C and sugar in the lemon juice to turn your markings a warm brown that is easy to mistake for dried blood.

13. It takes about thirty seconds before you will see any color change in the text, so use that to build the drama. Act disappointed when nothing happens immediately, and chant more frantically. After around 45 seconds, your friend will notice the three words you treated with lemon juice darkening. Act as though you don't notice; make your friend point them out to you.

14. Act surprised, then ask your friend to turn over the card under his/her hand. Alleluia! It's the card. Take the iron from your friend. *Turn it off, unplug it,* and put it in a place where it won't burn the hotel down or be touched by anyone inclined to frivolous legal action.

15. Rip out the page of the bible and give it to your friend as a souvenir. Remember, the book is your own property, so you're not thwarting the Gideons' self-righteous intentions by mutilating the missionary bunk they're trying to ram down your throat.

EVERLASTING LIES

Here are some variations and fine touches to enhance your performing experience:

✝ Sneak a prepared bible into your friend's room and do the trick there. Nobody can tell one Gideon bible from another. It makes it more amazing if you're using a "borrowed" book.

✝ The bible is equipped to provide punch lines for other Heart cards (alas, the unforesightful prophets totally omitted any reference to "Spades," "Clubs,"and "Diamonds"). Here's where to find some other Hearts:

Two of Hearts: Joshua 7: verses 3, 4, and 5

Seven of Hearts: Leviticus 26: verses 21, 30, 36

Eight of Hearts: Luke 2: verses 21, 34, 35 (good for christmas)

✝ The bible is loaded with blunt messages you can materialize for irritating friends. Get out your iron and pretend to use your Gideon as a Magic 8-ball. Got a houseguest who has overstayed the welcome? Paint your lemon juice on Proverbs 25:17, "Withdraw thy foot from thy neighbor's house; lest he be weary of thee and so hate thee." The bible provides enjoinders against almost anything you can name. Prophets don't approve of much.

✝ Whenever you stay in a hotel room, order your tea with lemon and prepare your bible to do the Revelation 17 card trick. If you don't get a chance to perform the trick yourself, leave your prepared bible behind, with a little pentacle drawn inside the back cover to identify it. Make a note of the room number, and next time call ahead to the front desk and make sure your target audience is booked in that room.

Even if you never intend to return to the hotel, gimmick your bible. Lots of people read our books. That means that over the years, your chances of walking into a hotel room that contains a prepared bible keep getting better. Just imagine someday spotting the pentacle on the bible in somebody's room and doing the trick with *no* possibility of preparation!

Of course, you mustn't molest real Gideon bibles. That would frustrate the sanctimonious meddling of the Gideons. Instead, you should fill your suitcases with hundreds of pounds of store-bought bibles to leave behind wherever you go.

That's our official advice. From here on, it's your clambake.

*We always keep a good stock of high-quality imitation Gideon bibles on hand.
It's an amazing coincidence: the number of bibles in our collection exactly equals
the number of hotels we've stayed at.*

TELL 'EM "PENN SAYS HI" — II

THINGS JUST KEEP GETTING BETTER. Fewer people in the world are starving. People live longer. More babies survive. The world gets cleaner, less violent, and more comfortable. We have more leisure time and we know more about ourselves and the universe. If you're sniffing around for a time to live, pick the future. Luckily, we're all going to live at least a little bit into the future, and we'll all live a little longer in the future, thanks to the future.

We don't really lose anything too good as we move ahead. We may get nostalgic for drive-in movies, but kids can certainly make out to Pay Per View. I always wanted to own an IBM Correcting Selectric II, but now I have a computer to write on, right on! Richard Feynman, Dean Martin, and John Lennon are dead, but technology has kept alive more of the good parts of them than we would have had if they had lived longer ago. Those very good parts will live on forever (or nearly close enough to forever for my taste).

In our last book, we wrote about buying Jell-O (and discussed the problems of the casual use of brand names — please consult *Penn & Teller's How to Play with Your Food* before using the name "Jell-O" for just any flavored gelatin dessert) for strangers. It's been reported that a few people who read that book have been buying flavored gelatin desserts for strangers and telling them, "Penn says hi." I hope that goes on forever. We're just a little obsessed with immortality.

There's another "Penn says hi" thing that I do, and you can do, but you won't be able to do it for very long into the future. Tollbooths are going to be history. This is our book and we're supposed to be able to do any stinkin' thing we want, but I don't think we should go into all the reasons that we believe roads should be privately owned. We probably shouldn't go into all the really cool technology that would allow us to really "pay as we go" without even stopping. We'll keep working for less and less government and more and more individual power, and maybe someday people instead of "the people" will own roads. It's not going to happen soon, but maybe someday some way. Before that happens, with government still owning roads, some of the cool technology will be implemented and toll booths will be things of the past. As a matter of fact, I know only a couple places (in FLA last I checked) where you still hand a quarter to someone in a booth to travel on a road or bridge. I guess it's hard to collect enough quarters an hour to make it worth paying someone to collect them.

Hey, if you happen to be going through a tollbooth, and it's cheap enough, and you have to be in the change lane anyway, give the toll collector double the toll and say, "This is for the car behind me. Tell 'em 'Penn says hi — work for world peace.'"

It's really fun, and you won't be able to do it much longer. But don't worry — we'll have even cooler things to do in the future. Things are just getting better.

A FLIGHT ATTENDANT CALLED "DAN"

A S WE WERE PREPARING THIS BOOK, Teller found himself seated next to an off-duty flight attendant on a cross-country flight. He asked the flight attendant for stories of novel passenger behavior you might enjoy emulating.

The flight attendant — let's call him Dan — told about his novice days on People Express, a now-defunct economy airline on which, to keep down expenses, flight attendants sold the tickets on board the plane while the flight was in progress. The flight attendant approached an attractive passenger and asked for her fare.

"I don't have money now. But come back later in the flight," she said with a charming smile.

Dan warned her that if she didn't pay, he'd have to alert security to meet her and take her into custody. She nodded cheerfully and told him not to worry.

During the flight, Dan noticed the woman strolling through the aisles of the plane, and here and there falling into conversation with men seated alone. A few minutes later, Dan observed that both the woman's seat and her new acquaintance's seat were empty. This phenomenon occurred several times during the flight.

Half an hour before the plane was to land, Dan returned to the woman and asked her for her fare. She paid in cash out of a huge wad of bills and even tipped Dan twenty bucks.

Teller thought this sounded like a great way to fly, but if you're cool enough to pull off that gag, you sure don't need our help. So Teller asked Dan for other suggestions.

Dan told him about an elderly Pakistani passenger who had never been on a plane before. The Pakistani gentleman heard the announcements coming over the P.A. system and assumed it was an intercom. So when he wanted a cup of coffee, he stood up and shouted his order into the ventilator nozzle.

Teller found this inspiring. So the next time he flew with Penn, he conspired with the flight attendant: she was to watch for Teller to stand up and shout into the ventilator nozzle, then bring him a cup of tea.

Teller waited an hour or so, then stood up and yelled into the vent, "May I have a cup of tea, please, with cream and sugar?" Moments later his nice hot drink arrived.

The photo is a re-enactment, depicting accurately the instant in which mild confusion turned to disgusted annoyance at Teller's attempt to play a joke on someone who knows him too well.

Maybe you would have better luck if you try it on a stranger.

Here's another re-enactment. Penn and Teller were flying first class and Teller noticed the little glass salt and pepper shakers they give you to spice up your tiny filet mignon. As he ate, Teller remembered the stinky pre-adolescent gag of filling the sugar bowl with salt. So, while Penn wasn't looking, he filled his own salt shaker with sugar, and when coffee came at the end of the meal, seasoned his own cup of coffee with "salt" and drank it with gusto.

As the photo shows: if you're reading this book to become more popular, you might as well put it down right now.

It's interesting that after we took all the trouble to dress up the windows of this bus to look like plane windows, we forgot to remove the little plaques with the bus emergency directions.

IN
THE
MÜTTER
MUSEUM

MY MOTHER RECALLS THAT ONE BRIGHT summer's afternoon in 1949, she left me alone for a few minutes in my crib in the nursery. Suddenly she heard me cooing delightedly. She hurried back in to see what was making me so happy.

I was sitting in a pool of blood. I had broken my bottle and cut myself on the glass. My mother screamed, but I was unperturbed. I was holding up a shard of glass in the sunlight and admiring the sparkling blood with a fascinated smile.

A morbid child, you say? Not at all. I saw the glitter and the color and recognized that I was holding something beautiful. Had I understood the danger, as my mother did, I might have cried. But I didn't know enough to be afraid. No doubt I thought that a quick sting was a small price for such beauty.

As I grew, I encountered many other beautiful, painful things: vibrant red nosebleeds, and golden, buzzing nests of yellow jackets.

Now, I'm an adult. I listen to fear and avoid pain. I take antihistamines and hire exterminators. Preventive medicine makes my life more pleasant, and consequently, a little less beautiful. That's why, every now and then, I visit the Mütter Museum. I love the Mütter because it stings.

The Mütter Museum lurks quietly behind a bronze plaque outside the wrought-iron gate at 19 South 22nd Street in Philadelphia, home of the College of Physicians of Philadelphia, an organization founded in 1787. Hipper and more egalitarian

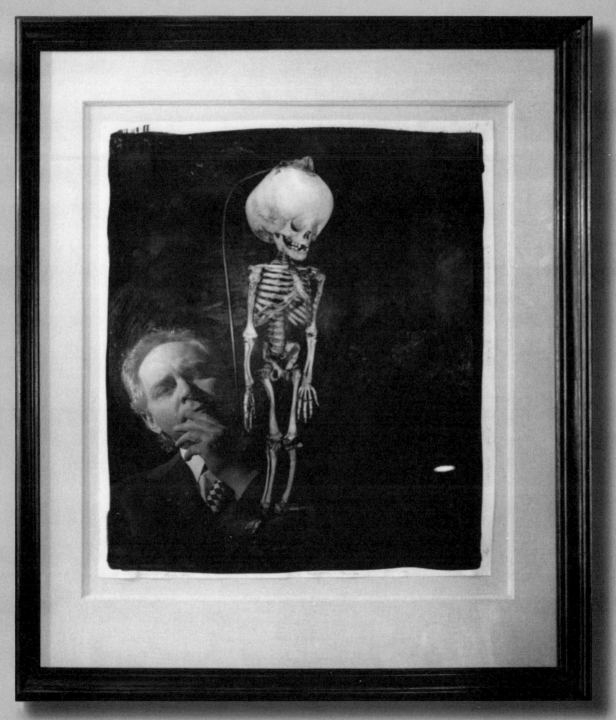

Skeleton No. 1 — "Onionhead"
©1985 Akin & Ludwig

than most private medical societies, the College invites not only doctors but the public to use its historical collections and its state-of-the art health archive, the C. Everett Koop Center. You can stroll through the College's gardens and smell the herbs from which doctors over the centuries made medicines (some worked, some didn't). In the College Gallery you can learn how discreet U.S. presidents have been about their health problems — you can even see the actual tumor that was removed from President Cleveland's jaw in a secret operation aboard a private yacht.

The Mütter Museum is deep in the bowels of the stern Georgian building. The Museum began as the "unwritten book" of Dr. Thomas Dent Mütter, a nineteenth-century surgeon who believed that text and diagrams were not enough to prepare medical students to confront Nature's disturbing departures from the norm. He started collecting and preserving things he wanted his students to see: tumors, aneurisms, bone pathologies (including a skeleton whose ribcage had been deformed by corseting), even the bladder stones removed from Chief Justice John Marshall — more than 1,700 pieces altogether. In 1858 he bequeathed his collection to the College, under whose care it has grown to more than 20,000 items, only a fraction of which are on view at any one time.

You enter the Mütter through a small gallery containing a reconstruction of an early twentieth century doctor's examination room — complete with enema cans and big needles for withdrawing fluids from body cavities. From here you are led to the mezzanine of a cavernous room two stories tall. You descend as you explore. The room is ringed with polished wooden display cases containing the collection. Thick burgundy curtains keep out the sunlight, and matching carpets muffle your footfall. Brass lamps with green glass shades evoke the days of gas lamps, and carefully placed spotlights illuminate the exhibits like sculpture.

Some *are* literally sculptures, made with flawless wax-museum realism. Look, for example, at the face of Madame Dimanche (Widow Sunday), a Parisian woman of the early nineteenth century. She looks like the kind of matron you'd expect to find haggling over the price of a carp, except that from her forehead protrudes a tumor in the shape of a horn some six inches long, curving downward and almost touching her chin. She lived as a bourgeois unicorn until the age of eighty, when she found a surgeon who was at last able to remove her trademark. I bet she missed it.

Nearby is another waxworks, a face blooming with nodular leprosy. Little pink cauliflowers sprout all over the cheeks and eyebrows. How I wish my Sunday School teacher had shown me this face. Her stories about miraculous cures would have meant something. I'd always pictured leprosy as a disease that merely made you look like Marcel Marceau.

Continue around the mezzanine and you encounter a wall of cases filled with skulls, 139 of them, collected by Dr. Joseph Hyrtl of Vienna and brought to the museum in 1874. Hyrtl, an anatomist, searched for correlations between the shape of a person's skull and his age, sex, occupation, and ethnic background. Each skull bears a label in faded ink, and each label suggests much in few words, like a poem. For example:

VIENNA

THEODOR PIRCHER, 29

CATHOLIC

PAINTER

SUICIDE BY POTASSIUM CYANIDE.

Poor Theodor! Only twenty-nine. Did your paintings not sell? Did you find the cyanide among your paints? And look, here's a young Romeo:

LINZ, UPPER AUSTRIA

SIMON JUHREN, 19

TAILOR

SUICIDE; HANGED HIMSELF BECAUSE
OF AN UNHAPPY LOVE AFFAIR.

I look down Hyrtl's 139 bony faces and they seem to be
saying to me: "Welcome to the family of man. And what shall
we write on *your* little label when *you* join us?"

Descend the stairs, and you find yourself greeted by a family of three skeletons. One is average adult height. One is 7'6",
the largest human skeleton on display in North America. One
is a 3'6" dwarf woman who worked in a house of prostitution
shortly before the Civil War. I look at the giant and the dwarf
side by side, and I can't help it: I think of Penn & Teller.

In a case beyond the skeletal trio is a head, sliced like
bread, with each slice in its own flat, sealed jar. At first I think,
ouch — a sliced head! Then I study it a little longer, and start
wondering how a pre-laser anatomist could cut so cleanly and
precisely that the folds of the brain, mazelike, are so neatly
intact.

A tall woman with a mane of auburn curls emerges from a
heavy oak door among the cases. This is Gretchen Worden, the
Mütter's director, who has, over my many visits, become my
friend. She's carrying a bottle of formaldehyde. I ask about the
head-slicing.

"It was frozen," she says in her low, vibrant voice, "no
small trick given turn-of-the-century refrigeration. And do you
know how they made these?" She points to a case containing
105 exquisite castings of the semi-circular canal of the ears of
creatures from man to elephant. I can't fathom how such things
could be made.

"Wax corrosions. Dr. Hyrtl — you know, from the skull

collection upstairs? — filled the cadaver's ear canal with wax, then used acids to corrode away the flesh and bone around it, leaving only the shape of the canal. Have you ever seen anything more delicate? It took him fourteen years to put this collection together." Gretchen glides away behind the heavy door.

Why do physicians spend so much time and trouble collecting? Because neither your suffering nor mine, viewed in isolation, does the human race much good. We are valuable to medicine only when we become part of a pattern. Come, look in this enormous jar: it's full of the brains of epileptics, collected in the hopes of finding a common trait that might be corrected surgically. Come, look under the stairs to the mezzanine. This huge chest of drawers contains more than 2,000 objects which Dr. Chevalier Jackson removed from the throats of choking victims — everything from nutshell to dentures to padlocks. And here is the log book in which Jackson recorded each case, how he treated it, and whether the patient survived (nearly all his patients lived, except when they sought help too late). To each of the victims, the choking was full of horror. But Jackson disciplined himself to see through the horror to the patterns behind it. What he learned enabled him to invent special instruments for removing foreign objects without surgery. We must be clinical only to be kind.

This leads us to the quietest corner of the museum, devoted to variations of childbirth. A chorus line of ten skeletons traces the normal infant's development from gestation to post-partum. Nearby stands the tiny skeleton of a pair of twins joined at the head and ribcage. Had they been my children, dead so young, I would have wept. But here, under glass, the twins simply look elfin, like a little pair of be-bop dancers in mid-swing.

Not many conjoined twins are allowed to remain so nowadays. We use modern surgery to "correct nature's mistake" at birth. In the late twentieth century we consider solitude our natural condition. Mates divorce, and even friendship is diag-

nosed as a disorder — co-dependency. So the concept of living
a life interlocked with another human is unthinkable.

But here at the Mütter I can look at the body cast of the
original Siamese Twins, Chang and Eng, taken after their autop-
sy in Philadelphia in 1874. And they seem to me not a "mistake" or a "disabled" person, but a super-being. They were
world-famous for their looks, just as fashion models and actors
are, and for their acrobatic talents. They fathered twenty-one
children and retired as gentlemen farmers. Would they have
been happier if they had been separated at birth and passed
their lives as, say, fishermen in drab anonymity?

I ask the question, but the twins remain silent. In fact, as I
look around, the entire museum is reticent, waiting to be looked
at, but unwilling to explain away its mystery. There are no bab-
bling pushbutton recorded explanations; even the labels are
terse and sometimes cryptic. And this is as it should be. For
these things around me are not textbook illustrations, but actual pieces of life suspended in a world beyond time, pain, and
passion. Like life, they are not inclined to explain themselves.
So we look, think, study, wonder. When school children enter
the Mütter, they instinctively start talking in whispers and
chewing their gum thoughtfully. Tattooed teenagers with nose
rings, who come to show how cool they can be in the face of
freaks and death, grow introspective when they realize that
what they are looking at is *real*, important, and very beautiful.

No one is quieter than the Soap Lady. She is a short, stout,
nude woman the color and texture of fallen leaves in November.
She has slept in a glass case at the Mütter since 1874. She was
fat, and when she was buried the temperature and moisture of
the grave were just right for causing her plump flesh to trans-
mute into adipocere, a soaplike substance. She led an undistin-
guished life, but now she is a star, having made her mark on the
world at the last possible moment — as she was decomposing.
Here, in the Mütter, she is celebrated, loved, and cared for.

I hope that, like the Soap Lady, my remains contain some rare pathology of which the Mütter needs a specimen. Nothing would please me more than spending my afterlife in a glass case in the distinguished company of Widow Sunday and Dr. Hyrtl's 139 bony friends — serving science and human curiosity, inspiring philosophic speculation, and making the faint-hearted shudder.

A DRUNK DRIVING TRICK

OH, CALM DOWN. JUST CALM DOWN. PENN & Teller are teetotalers. No higher power. No 12-Step. We're not recovering anything. We don't have a drinking problem and we never did. It's easy — we *never* drink and we *never* do drugs. Never. We don't just avoid inhaling, we don't get near drugs. Since none of our friends do drugs, it's unlikely we would ever be in the room with boring hippies toking up, but if we were and they handed us one of those marijuana cigarettes that every generation has its own special name for, we would say, "No, we don't do drugs, hippie loser." How hard is that? You would think a latent presidential human being would have at least that much backbone. We're the only ones that believed him when he said he didn't inhale, and that's the only time we believed him. He believed that *pretending* to do drugs to please people is the kind of character trait the United States wants in a president. And he was right.

One of us never even tasted alcohol, and neither of us has ever used any recreational drugs other than caffeine and nicotine. We use decaffeinated everything, but it still sneaks in, and nicotine, well, jeez, there are just so many cool cigarette tricks. Yes, we have smoked and do smoke onstage, but not in our real life. So there. All that being said, we have a drunk driving trick.

The antidrinking and antidrug people always play that goody-goody thing. It makes us crazy. Being stone cold sober all the time is not an easy-listening thing to do. As a matter of fact, it's damn antisocial. "Just say no" is stupid. It should be, "Just say no, you boring, hippie throwback." The only clear-eyed role model we had as kids was Frank Zappa. He was wild and hated drugs. There's nothing better.

                        *   *   *
                       ** ** **

When we first started to kinda sorta hit Off Broadway, we were asked to do "Don't Drink and Drive" Public Service Announcements. We were really jazzed. We were excited to get bad-attitude sobriety out to the masses. We wrote several ads. One of the best was a straight address to camera, Teller, with an abundance of appropriate props and attitude, and Penn saying, "If your friend wants to drive drunk — take his car keys . . . and while you're at it — take his wallet — he won't notice — he's drunk!" They liked that one. We had another; once again, with Teller propping and emoting, Penn said, "If you're going to kill someone — use a knife — then you can pick who you want to kill and you can enjoy it. Don't drive drunk." They didn't like that one, but they were forced to at least consider it.

We were all jacked up to tape these when we found out some of the money for the production was from the United Council of Churches or something like that. Well, we don't truck with them cats — they drink wine and stuff. So, outside of a thrown together version for some PBS New Year's fund-raiser thing, we never did our anti-drunk-driving ads. If you happen to be a teetotaling Atheist with some coin to put into PSAs, give us a call — our time, image, and ideas will be free for the cause.

As much as we liked the idea, it never occurred to us that it could be a trick. When we went to the Net to find ideas for this book, one of our favorite fans, Georgia Maher, known in the ether as TexasArtChick, told us about a trick she does. Coincidentally, it was the real-world equivalent of our own little PSA ideas. Ms. Maher is a wild artist in Texas with photo-realist paintings she did of the Three Stooges all over her computer and her large portraits of Penn & Teller that ooze blood.

Georgia, being a teetotaler, always winds up being the designated driver. Many guests hitch rides to parties, knowing that the Texas Art Chick will get them home safe and sound. The system isn't perfect. Every so often a drunken jerk (redundant) would drive his or her own car, expecting to drive home after a night of "partying." Georgia, like all the goody-goodies say you should, would try to take the car keys.

Sometimes this works, but often the loadie just gets angry, and who wants to try to take keys away from a combative boozer? (It's *so* hard to remember that saving the juicehead's life is an unwanted byproduct of trying to save innocent motorists. Try to keep looking on the bright side: Even without his or her keys the rummy could fall down the stairs and/or choke on his or her own vomit.)

Georgia, being a Penn & Teller fan, devised a sneaky little way around wrestling with sots. It's great: you also get to have fun and practice your sleight of hand. Alkies are easy marks. If you can't scam a barfly, you should read our books as fiction and forget the tricks.

Before you do this trick, play fair. Give the potential vehicular murderer a chance to do the right thing. Mention that maybe you

should drive the lush home. If he or she refuses, don't argue. It's time for the Georgia technique. Find a time to cop the keys from pocket, purse, or fanny pack. It shouldn't take much, just steal buzzy's keys whenever you get the chance. As we point out in our PSA, it's also a jolly good time to cop some cash. This is a trick you can and should be paid for. Now, a very self-righteous person (is it possible to be more self-righteous than us?) might just throw the keys down the nearest sewer. That's okay, but Georgia's trick is a little more fun. Here's what you do. Find a private location that doesn't have the reek of alcohol vomit, take the ignition key off the ring, and replace it with a similar key. Don't try to put the keys back on the bush-league Bukowski's person — you've already been too close to the smelly bagged barbarian — instead, leave the keys somewhere to be discovered. The blitzed mark will think he or she just dropped the keys during a boiled owl stagger.

When it's time for the lubricated loser to head home, don't argue much, just watch and enjoy. Watch the rumbag try to drive home and fail. If it's a foreign car, the wino won't even be able to get in the door. If the three sheets to the wind mark decides to sleep over, just switch the keys back during the coma sleep of the obfuscated fool.

Georgia, always helpful, offers to try the keys herself and, of course, fails as well. If Mr. or Ms. Plastered then lets her drive them home, she has the keys in her possession and can switch them back in the bathroom right before leaving. She hands over the keys when leaving off dipso at his or her home, with an "Oh, don't forget these!" By the time your schnockered scumbag wakes up, he, she, or it has working keys.

◄ *There should probably have been a photograph of one of us switching keys,*
  while the other one staggers to his car, but neither of us would debase ourselves
by even pretending to be drunk. So we commissioned Georgia to draw this picture
with a drunken model.

Georgia is very serious about this; she buys dummy keys at junk shops and flea markets and carries them to parties. We might be tempted to just carry a file, and file off a bump on the key and be done with it, but that would be unkind to a person that was willing to take other people's lives into his or her incompetent, stinko, shaking hands.

A really good person could buy a few blank masters and have them cut at random. It really is a pretty cheap investment (you know the tangle-footed elbow-bender will unknowingly reimburse you for your key costs plus your time, skill, this book, *and* a modest profit). For what you get out of it — magic practice, torture of an annoying guzzler, pocket money . . . and . . . oh, yeah, safer roads for innocent travelers, it's a pretty good deal.

IF IT FOOLED EINSTEIN,
IT MIGHT FOOL
YOUR BRAINY FRIENDS, TOO
(A Trick That Travels Light)

THE LATE AL KORAN, A MAGICIAN renowned for subtle psychology, was performing at the Savoy Hotel in London. He was doing his version of the mathematical miracle you're about to learn. Albert Einstein was in the audience. After the show, Einstein confidentially took Koran aside to ask him if the trick involved hiding coins "up his sleeve." Koran denied it and repeated the trick, clearly with no assistance from his wardrobe. He fooled Einstein a second time. "It's not the numbers," Koran told the great mathematician reassuringly, "it's the words that fooled you."

The right words can give you the power to slip through the cracks in another person's intellect and make him or her believe a lie. Even great thinkers sometimes have those cracks. Alexander Graham Bell learned that the word "lunacy" is derived from the Latin word *luna* (moon). The idea got under his skin. So whenever there was a full moon, he found himself pulling curtains and setting up screens to keep the moon from creeping up on him and his family and driving them mad with its noxious light. In some part of his mind, I'm sure the great inventor knew better. But that single word "lunacy" had wriggled into a crack.

There are good lies and bad ones. When you lie while doing a magic trick, everybody knows you are lying and there's no harm done. Al Koran's lies were good. Hitler's were not. So we'll teach you to lie like Al Koran, and so expertly that you, too, will fool illuminati.

This is the perfect trick for those who travel light. Some of our other stunts require special gimmicks (and, dammit, they're all worth lugging). But all the tools you need for this one you can carry in your head.

HOW IT LOOKS

The ideal setting for this trick is a gambling casino. Let's imagine you're on vacation in Las Vegas, and your friend is playing the slot machines, and toting around a plastic bucket full of quarters.

You look at your friend's lucre-bucket and say, "Did you ever try those contests where you try guessing how many gumballs are in a jar?" It's good to ask questions when you're setting someone up for a hoax. It gets your victim's attention, and makes your devious premeditation less apparent.

Nod enthusiastically at whatever your friend answers and continue, "Well, when I was a kid I got good at guessing how much loose change people had in their hands. I wonder if I can still do it. Let's try. I'll turn my head away and you take a handful of coins out of your bucket. Don't let me see how many you take."

Your friend does so. "Now I'll do the same," you say, and do.

Tell your friend to count his/her coins silently while you count yours.

"Now," you say, "don't let me see how many you have, but hold your handful of coins up to my ear and jingle them." You listen intently. Then you jingle your own coins next to your ear and appear to be thinking hard.

"Okay," you say, "I have as much money as you do."

You jingle your own coins some more and listen. "No, wait: I have four pesky extra quarters."

You continue to jingle the coins and listen and furrow your brow as if calculating, and add, "And enough left

over to bring your total to $4.25. You don't believe that, do you? Let me listen again."

You listen to both fists again and say, "Yup, I think I'm right. As much as you, four irritating extra quarters, and enough left over to make yours $4.25. Let's see how close I came. How much do you have?"

Imagine your friend says $2.50.

You count out ten quarters. Your first statement is true.

Now you count out and discard those four vexing "extras." Your second statement is true, too.

Now you say, "You say you have $2.50. I said I would have enough left over to bring your total to $4.25. Count your money onto the table."

When your friend reaches $2.50, you continue with the quarters you have in your hand, counting aloud, "$2.75, $3, $3.25, $3.50, $3.75, $4 and ..." dramatically opening your hand to drop out the last quarter, "$4.25."

You are dead on. Your friend is amazed at the batlike precision of your ears.

HOW DID YOU KNOW
HOW MUCH
YOUR FRIEND HAD?

You didn't. It was a rhetorical trick. Here's how it works:

1. Have your friend take "a handful" of coins. "Handful" suggests more than a few but not too many. You need to be sure she/he leaves enough quarters behind to allow *you* to take even more. (For the moment, assume your friend is cooperative and doesn't take the whole bucketful; later we'll tell you how to deal with a greedy person.)

2. Take about ten more than you estimate your friend has. Just look at your friend's closed hand. If it's *very* full, make yours fuller.

3. While your friend counts his/her money, count yours. Let's say you count twenty-one quarters, $5.25. Mentally divide your take into two parcels, a large and a small (in our example, we divide $5.25 into $4.25 plus "four pesky extra quarters").

4. Go through the business of listening to the coins. This is all window dressing, but as far as your audience is concerned, this is the big moment when the trick happens. Make it look hard.

5. Now, you are going to tell your friend the simple truth ("I have $5.25") but you're going to phrase it to *seem* as if you know how many she/he has.

   Start by declaring, "I have as much money as you do." Well, of course you do. You took more. But act as though you just learned it from the jingling.

6. Listen to your coins again and, as if correcting yourself, say, "No, wait — I have four pesky extra quarters ... " Of course you have four extras. You took at least ten more than your friend.

7. Continue to jingle and listen as if refining your estimate further, and add, " ... and enough left over to bring your total to $4.25."

   Now, you really haven't said much. It's no surprise that $5.25 is $4.25 plus four quarters. That's just arithmetic. And as long as your friend took less than $4.25, of *course* you have as much money as he/she does "plus enough left over to make $4.25." Confused? Try this. Hold up any number of fingers. I predict that I'm holding up as many as you, plus enough to make thirteen. Now turn the page.

See? Same principle.

8. By telling about your childhood skill, then jingling the coins and listening so carefully, you make your victim *expect* you to know how much money she/he has taken. Then you make three confusing statements, prove them all true, and take a big bow. If you do it with enough bravado, the geniuses will miss the fact that your statements prove nothing except that you know how much is in *your own* hand.

This is a fallacy of logic called "assuming the conclusion" — the same bluff the politician uses when he/she says, "Public school children can't read; therefore we need to raise taxes." The first part may be true, but it doesn't prove the second.

If this trick fooled the man who invented the Special Theory of Relativity, there's a good chance it will fool even your smartest friends. They're probably less good at math than Einstein, and it's a safe guess that if they're playing slot machines, they're suckers for moonshine.

TIPS

1. If you're good at palming, this stunt can be profitable even if you blow the trick.

2. Though this trick is superb with coins, you can also use the principle to improvise any time you have a lot of little some-things (toothpicks, aspirins, after-dinner mints). Just make sure your friend leaves enough behind so that you can take more. You adjust your talk, as, for example, "I have as many tooth-picks as you do, six tedious extras, and enough left over to make your total twenty-eight."

3. What if your friend takes too many coins, so that he/she hasn't left enough for you to be able to take more? No problem. As soon as you notice that too many are missing for the trick to work, say to your friend, "Good. Now, a few at a time, start putting them back in the bucket." Wait until there are enough to make the trick possible, then say, "Now, any time you want, stop. Are you satisfied with your choice?" As far as your friend's concerned, this is just a slightly eccentric procedure for making a random selection. As far as you're concerned, this saves your pitiful ass.

4. You can repeat this trick, but be sure to vary the number of "extras." Just remember to subtract whatever you're calling "extras" from your total.

5. An unscrupulous person might turn this lovely and mystifying conundrum into a bet and quickly make back the price of this book. He/she might propose, "If I'm wrong, I pay you double. If I'm right, I get to keep all the money." Anyone who stoops to such chiseling should be punished by sending a check for half the take to:

> Penn & Teller
> Box 377
> 4132 S. Rainbow Blvd.
> Las Vegas, NV 89103

I AM THE GOD OF CARBONATION

DO YOU HAVE ANY IDEA HOW MANY MAGIC books Teller reads? I mean do you have *any* idea? Well, I don't — but it's a lot. He wades through the mind-numbingly bad writing, confusing directions, and the zillions of tricks that just plain don't work. And what does he get out of it? How many tricks out of these books end up in the Penn & Teller show? Well, two, but Teller had to reinvent how to do them.

The following is a great trick that appeared in A-1 Multimedia's *The Art of Astonishment* by Paul Harris with additional writing by Eric Mead. I've seen Eric doing great close-up magic at "The Tower, Comedy Magic Bar" in Snowmass right outside of Aspen, Colorado. I believe it's the best place in the world to see card tricks while suffering from altitude sickness. If you go and tip well, say we sent you.

Paul and Eric came up with the only trick in *How to Play in Traffic* that I actually do. You won't see me soaping up mirrors, writing card trick luv faxes, or going to prison for a computer gag, but I actually do this Eric and Paul trick. I have said, in my own personal life, "Hey, want to see a trick?" and I've done this trick. I've done it out of my working suit, in real life, in my civvies, as a citizen.

This is probably the easiest trick in the book and it kills. It baffles. I have to give it a big buildup, because if I just tell you how it's done, you're going to think that it wouldn't fool anyone. It's that simple. Goddamn, this trick is easy. I mean, man, you don't need anything. The first time you *think* about this trick, you can be performing it in front of people.

Here's a list of the props:

2 cans of soda pop

They don't even have to be the same brand or flavor of soda. Here's the preparation:

Finish reading this article.

You don't even have to read all the mind-numbingly bad writing, you can just skip right to the confusing directions. You don't really even have to read it. You can ask someone else to read it and tell you the secret.

The sodas aren't gimmicked or prepared in any way, and they don't have to match. You can do it fresh out of an hotel mini-bar or straight out of a gas station soda machine. It's a miracle and it takes *no work*. What the hell more could you want?

I'll tell you what the hell more you could want; you could want it to be really messy and humiliating for the other person. Your wish is granted — it can be that. I'll tell you what else the hell more you could want; you could want it to be just a good laugh and do no harm to anyone (why the hell would you want that?). That, too — it can be that. It can be either, it all depends on the kind of soda. Use cola beverages and it'll sticky up the whole area for days. Use seltzer or club soda and it'll clean up with, well, with a little club soda.

This is a perfect trick. When it's time to share a canned soft drink with someone (maybe some of our readers would want to do it alone, but I don't want to think about that), say, out of the blue, "*I am the God of Carbonation!* I have total power over dissolved CO_2. It's supernatural, but it's not that useful. It's more useful than the supernatural ability to bend spoons, but still not that useful."

(Never pass up a chance to take a shot at phony psychics. "Phony psychics" is, of course, redundant, but that's covered in our other books.)

Your friend may question your claim to the God of Carbonation title. It doesn't matter what she or he says. You continue, "Listen, pick any two cans of soda you want — any two. Go ahead, pick two." (The God of Carbonation is easily excitable and rather pushy).

Don't touch the cans. Hold your hands in the international "I'm not touching the cans" position.

Tell your friend to pick either of the cans and shake it up and down really, really hard. Encourage him or her to shake the livin' bejesus out of the can.

No matter how much and how hard they shake, shame them into shaking more. You want them to shake it up and down a good nine or ten times. "My grandmother can shake soda cans better than that and she's dead," would be the kind of witty remark you might want to use to egg them on.

Tell them you're going, for the first time, to touch the soda cans, and caution them to keep track of the shaken can. I don't know how you're perceived in your peer group, but when a nut like me is holding something that is as potentially explosive as a shook soda can, I have my audience's full attention. Hold the just shaken can up to the shaker's ear so he or she can hear the little bomb a-fizzin'. That way they know it's not a dud.

"I am the God of Carbonation. I will take the agitated CO_2 from this abused can and move it to the Can of Peace."

It doesn't matter *what* you do here, but you have to do something. Make your movements very crisp, even, and gentle, don't shake either can. Be very careful. It's a good idea to switch hands, but be very careful not to let the fish lose track of the shaken can. They must know which is which. It helps the trick if you turn the cans upside down once, very slowly, and then right them again, but don't let it look like you're shaking either.

Hand the *unshaken* can to your friend. Take the can that remains in your hand and make sure your friend knows it's the *shaken* one. Say something like, "This is the can that was shaking like Katharine Hepburn, right?" When you are sure that they are sure that it's the can they shook, look at the shaken can beatifically and say, "It is now at peace." Quickly stick the can near your victim's face and open it.

Nothing happens, the can *was* at peace. It doesn't overflow, not even a little. You are the God of Carbonation.

Now for the punch line.

Take the *unshaken* can back and say, "This is the placid can. The can which absorbed the troubles of the disturbed can. This is the turbulence-sucking Can of Peace." (You don't have to memorize any of this, you can just make it up as you go. That's what I'm doing.) "Here *you* open it, I'll hold it."

As soon as he or she lifts the flip top on the stagnant can — *it explodes.* It explodes all over them. It explodes with such force that it

sucks the sides of the can in as it explodes. "It's the Second Law of Carbodynamics — fizz cannot be created or destroyed, but the God of Carbonation can move the fizz at will," you brag. If you're drinking seltzer or club soda, you both have a good laugh. If you're drinking full-tilt sugar cola, well, you'll have to wash your hand and the sap will be sticky until bath and laundry day.

It's a great trick. It really is. It's mind-boggling. Did you use incredible sleight of hand to switch the cans? Did you put a tiny release hole in the can with your specially groomed and reinforced heavy metal fingernail?

No, there's nothing that hard about it.

Here's the secret — you squeeze the unshaken can as it's opened.

That's the only secret. Nothing else to it. Don't be disappointed — it's not bad news, it's good news. It's a great trick and there's no work. I don't know why it works. I don't know why the shaken can doesn't explode. I guess they've changed the way they package soda or something. No matter how hard you shake a soda can it takes only about twenty seconds for it to completely calm down. No one we asked knew that. I wouldn't try the trick on soda can designers, but I don't think anyone else knows. As long as your God of Carbonation ritual takes twenty seconds or more, the shaken can will not explode. Make sure you hold the can straight up, perpendicular to the ground, and open it all the way with one quick action. That'll get rid of any little bit of fizz that didn't calm down in the twenty seconds.

When they start to open the still can, just squeeze the aluminum side and it'll spurt like Ol' Faithful. Squeeze it on the side that's away from the audience, as hard as you can, with your thumb. Start squeezing before it's opened. Tilt the can towards them so there's no room for air at the top of the can. Make sure if that fizz wants out, it needs to take liquid with it. As soon as he or she has opened the can just a little crack, and it starts exploding — pull it away. Stop the victim from opening it further. This will give you the most force through the smallest opening, and that's what you and the Jet Propulsion Lab want. The little opening and the tilting are refinements. All you really need to know is *squeeze the can*. Stop squeezing before the side they can see gets dented. The can will be a dented wreck, but the misdirection of soda all over your audience will give you time to heave it in a trash can. Even if they dig in the trash and examine it, it's no big deal — it just looks like the huge explosion sucked in the sides a little.

It fools people, it gets them sticky, and it's no work. It's a great trick. I just wish I could have worked in a James Bond "shaken not stirred" reference, but I just couldn't. I'm the God of Carbonation, not the god of segues.

THE CUPS AND BALLS

THIS IS JOHANN NEPOMUK HOFZINSER. IN 1854 Johann and his wife, Wilhemine, rented a posh suite in an exclusive neighborhood of Vienna. They furnished it with velvet sofas, Persian carpets, and trapdoors. They then began to hold regular open houses they called "Moments of Deception." The capacity of their living-room theatre was about twenty, and the admission price was outrageous.

For the next ten years, Viennese high society flocked to the
Hofzinser soirees. At Hofzinser's command, eggs danced to the
music of a small chamber ensemble. When he made tissue paper
butterflies, they came to life and fluttered around the room. Your
ring might vanish from Dr. Hofzinser's manicured fingertips and
reappear in the mouth of a live goldfish, swimming in a bowl. When
Johann held a mirror before your eyes, he could make you see a
vision of a rose which changed color and then emerged real and fra-
grant into your hand.

Hofzinser was a master of sleight of hand. The card tricks he
created were so difficult that few magicians of today attempt them.
His Cups and Balls — the ancient trick in which small balls teleport
from one cup to another — had a virtuosic twist. He used cups the
size of milkshake cans and at the end lifted them to reveal golden
birdcages with live canaries inside.

When I was in my early twenties, I went through my Hofzinser
period. I wore my hair long, listened to Strauss, sported brocaded
vests, and said, "*Nicht wahr?*" a lot. And, in emulation of my idol, I
decided to come up with my own routine for the Cups and Balls. I
read exhaustively about the trick, and practiced and experimented
wherever I went.

Whenever I saw three mysterious-looking cups, I bought them.
I bought silver goblets that rang like bells when struck with a wand.
On a cruise in Greece, I haggled for tiny cups of gilded lead and
practiced on the plane all the way home. I even designed three cups
modeled after an old Bosch print and had them carved from wood.

I remember an eerie moment in my Cups and Balls practice. I
was sitting under an umbrella at a burger stand, with three Styro-
foam coffee cups inverted on the table and three napkin balls rolled
up on top. I was not doing the trick, just staring at the cups and
ruminating as I sucked on my milkshake. A six-year-old boy wandered over and pointed at my props. "Magic?" he asked. I still
wonder: How did he know? Had he seen the trick on TV? Or is
there something about three cups and three balls that says "magic"
to our very DNA?

When I announced a vacation trip to England, my magician

friends told me to be sure to ring up Bob Read,* the world's fore-most collector of Cups and Balls engravings and memorabilia.

When I arrived in London, I phoned Bob and declared my passion for the Cups and Balls. That was all it took. "Hotels are expensive," Bob declared. "Stay at our place. No trouble. We insist."

---

* By day Bob is a press agent for the wool industry, and by night a magician apt to turn a card trick into a songfest of his favorite 1940s big-band jazz tunes, or slip his bowler hat under the back of his coat and render an impromptu impression of the Hunchback of Notre Dame.

I arrived in the evening. Bob and his consort, Pauline, greeted me with a key to their house and an invitation to use their digs as my own. Since it was late and they both had to work in the morning, they gave me the quick tour (pointing out essentials such as where the digestive biscuits and tea were kept) and led me to their guest room, a library with a fold-out couch. Then they went to bed.

I, being a jet-lagged night owl, was far from sleepy. I considered browsing the books in the library/guest room, but I'm leery of touching a book-collector's prize possessions. How would I entertain myself until I was ready to sleep? Of course! I would practice the Cups and Balls. I rolled up facial tissues to use as balls and found three dusty aluminum cups on the library shelf. That was all I needed. The tissue balls were hard to palm, and the aluminum cups felt cheesy and too big for my hands. But I thought it would do me good to practice with junk props, as runners strengthen themselves by strapping lead weights to their ankles.

When I got up the next noon, Bob and Pauline had already left for their day jobs. I had some biscuits and tea, left a thank-you note on the refrigerator, and went sightseeing. That night, when I got back, they were already asleep. I scarfed another snack, left another note, and retired to another all-night Cups-and-Balls session in the library. The all-night practicing was producing good results. I started to think that if I ever actually saw Bob and Pauline again, I'd try my routine out on them.

But for three days the pattern continued. My hosts were gone in the morning, and in bed before I got home at night. Night after night I practiced, and day after day I left notes. On the third night I found a note from Pauline, asking whether I was actually visiting or just sneaking in to put memos on their fridge.

The fourth day was a Saturday, and Bob and Pauline were home when I stumbled out of bed at half past noon. They made me eggs and bacon and brown toast and marmalade and a nice strong pot of tea. Then Bob offered to show me his Cups and Balls collection.

He pulled up a chair for me at the dining room table and brought out his prints, paintings, cartoons, and engravings by the hundreds — the booty of decades of visits to Portobello Road's antique shops. Among the rarest papers, Bob pointed out a letter.

It was from Keith Clark, a sleight of hand artist of the 1930s and '40s. The letter authenticated a set of antique cups he was selling from his personal collection. Clark said these cups had originally been made for Johann Nepomuk Hofzinser. What a treasure this letter was! Keith Clark had actually owned Hofzinser's cups.

"Does anyone know where they are today?" I asked.

"Sure," said Bob. "They're in my library. Didn't you see them? Funny how much they look like aluminum. But they're not. I've had them tested. They're some sort of light alloy that doesn't tarnish and . . ."

The blood was rushing through my ears too fast to hear anymore. I had been practicing every night with three wadded-up snot rags and three Holy Grails. No wonder I was starting to get good.

I hope Bob and Pauline stay at my house someday. I recently bought the Shroud of Turin, and I'm hemming it to use as a bath towel in the guest room.

Sorry, we're not teaching you the Cups and Balls. It would kill our shot at the best-seller list. We'd fill a tome explaining it, and you'd spend a decade learning it — even if you practiced with Hofzinser's cups.

YEAH, SURE, IT'S FOR MENDING

FOR YOUR COVENIENCE IN NOMADIC flimflam, we have — at considerable expense — arranged for small magic sets to be placed in the bathrooms of virtually all first-class hotels. To prevent the uninitiated from recognizing them, we have disguised our magic sets to look like this:

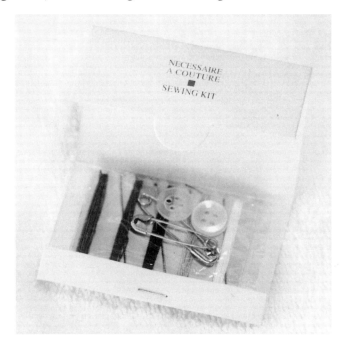

The Penn & Teller Magic Set

Convincing, eh? It looks like a sewing kit. Of course, a moment's reflection will make it obvious it must be a fake. People who book suites at the Four Seasons or the Ritz-Carlton don't darn their own socks.

Nonetheless, your secret is safe. This kit is a magic set only to those in the know, among whom you are about to be numbered.

1. LINT FROM HELL

Choose a color of thread that contrasts with the shirt, jacket, or dress you're wearing. Now, use the needle to thread it through the shoulder of the garment. Adjust the thread so that only a little end of it sticks out on the outside, and the rest hangs freely on the inside.

Now find your way into the company of a fastidious colleague. Wait. It won't be long before the person spots the untidy speck on your shoulder and helpfully plucks it off. As he/she pulls, the thread keeps coming.

You look inside your apparel and cry, "Good god! You've just unraveled my underwear!"

NOTE: If you want to invest in a more extravagant version of this, buy a whole spool of thread and put it in an inner pocket. It will supply yards and yards of fun.

2. OFF THE CUFF

This is Max Malini, a magician who traveled the world in the 1920s, armed with a few props, a snappy wardrobe, and limitless nerve.

Wherever he went, he would loiter in the poshest hotel lounges, making friends, doing tricks, and hobnobbing colorfully until some John D. Rockefeller or J. Pierpont Morgan took a liking to him and hired him for a private party. He ended up working for everybody from Teddy Roosevelt to the King of Siam.

A short, portly man with a mug like Nosferatu and a deep guttural voice with a heavy foreign accent, he had the gift of gall. He addressed King Edward VII of England as "Royal Mister," and Ed laughed and offered him a cigar. When a hostess

"Honest to Goodness, I only cheat a little."
—Malini

exclaimed that Malini had gouged her precious Louis Quatorze table while performing his card-stabbing routine, Malini pointed proudly to the damage and said, "You may say that mark was made by Max Malini." When a client who had booked him for a full-evening show was startled to find only Malini and a small suitcase instead of the truckload of tigers, assistants, and glitter boxes she expected, Malini declared, "I am the show."

One of his favorite impromptu stunts was biting a button off somebody's clothes, then restoring it instantaneously. Your Penn & Teller Magic Set equips you to follow in Malini's occlusion.

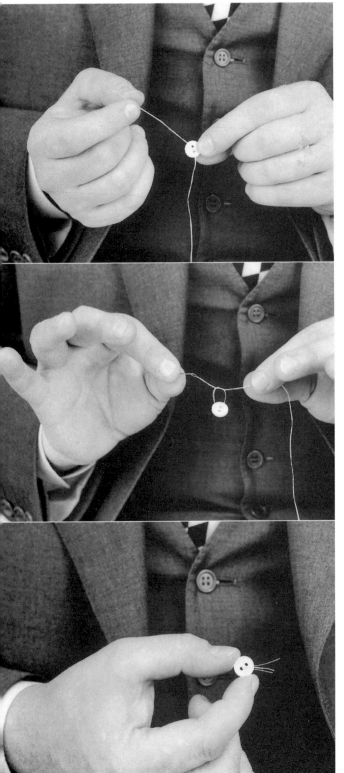

Take out the button and the needle threaded with white cotton. Run the thread through the button several times until it's well attached.

Then tie a little knot in your thread.

And tear off the rest of the thread raggedly, leaving an ugly, torn stub of thread.

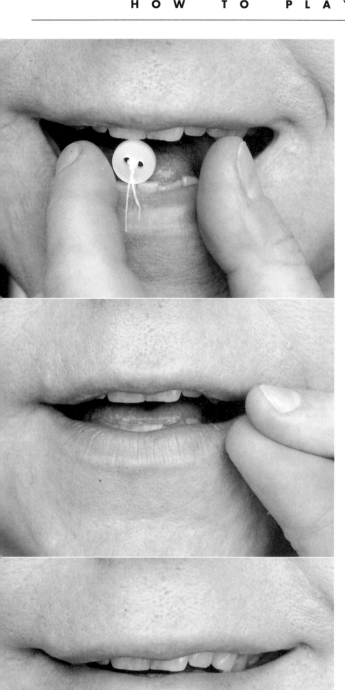

Now, wash it thoroughly, dry it, wrap it in a facial tissue, and put it in a clean pocket.

When you spot a person wearing a long-sleeved shirt whose buttons match your prepared button, go to a quiet, lonely place and put the button in your mouth, under your lower lip or wherever you can lodge it comfortably and securely.

WARNING: Do not try this if you have any trouble keeping a button securely under your lip. If there is the slightest possibility you might lose control and swallow, inhale, bite, or choke on the goddamned button, turn to another part of this book that requires less oral dexterity.

Return to the victim. Chat. In the middle of a thought, stop abruptly and look down at his/her cuff and say in a helpful tone, "Hold still. You've got a loose thread. Let me fix it."

Grip the person's sleeve like this, covering the cuff button with your thumb.

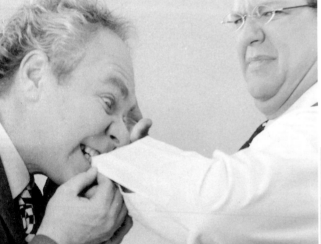

With your teeth nip a bit of the fabric near the cuff button. Pull the fabric taut, as if the button is resisting being bitten off. Then let the fabric snap free of your teeth.

Immediately display the button in your mouth.

Don't do this trick on dates or job interviews. It does not make you look attractive. It makes you look like Max Malini.

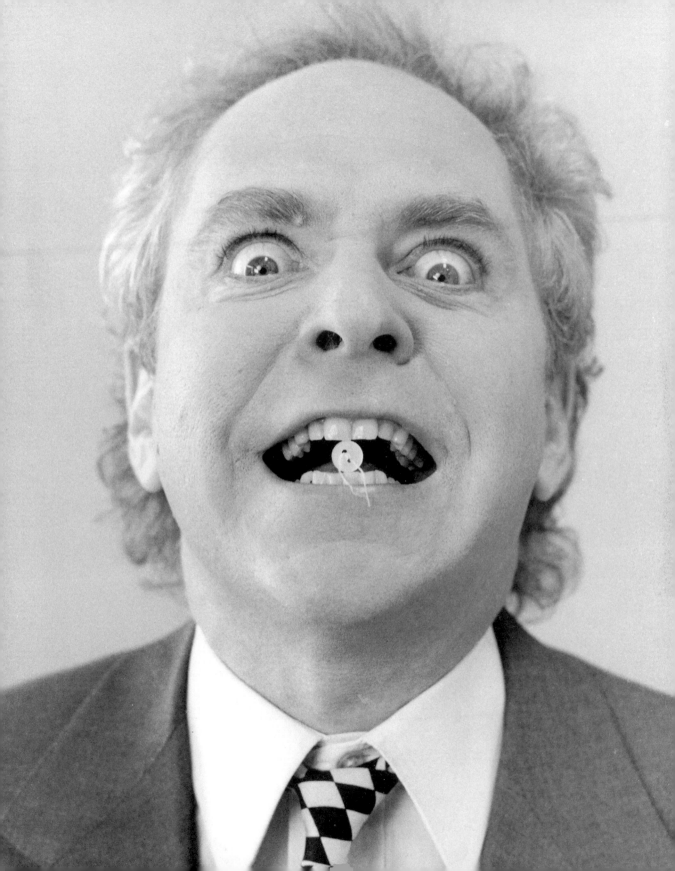

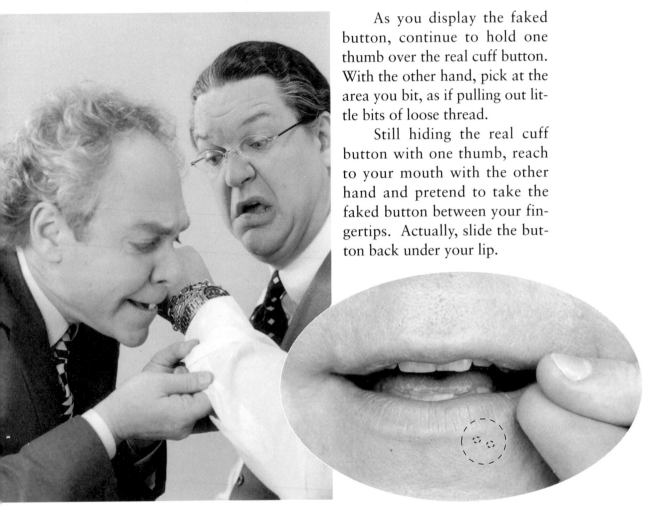

Button slides back here.

As you display the faked button, continue to hold one thumb over the real cuff button. With the other hand, pick at the area you bit, as if pulling out little bits of loose thread.

Still hiding the real cuff button with one thumb, reach to your mouth with the other hand and pretend to take the faked button between your fingertips. Actually, slide the button back under your lip.

Bring the imaginary button down to the cuff and simultaneously slide your thumb off the real one. Grip the real one in the fingertips that supposedly contain the mouth-button. Allow people to see the edges of the button as you press and rub it "onto" the fabric.

Display the "restored" button matter-of-factly, as if this is the way you always make sewing repairs, and pick up the conversation where it left off.

When Malini bit a button off President Warren G. Harding, he made the front pages of all the Washington newspapers. We provide the Penn & Teller Magic Set in the hopes that you, too, will someday bite a president.

Malini memorabilia courtesy of the American Museum of Magic.

NASA'S SUCCESSFUL QUANTIFYING OF COMEDY TIMING

BUDDY HACKETT SAID, "ASK ME WHAT'S THE secret of comedy."

Johnny Carson started to say, "What's the secret of . . . " and Buddy yelled, "Timing," very loudly, right in his face. It killed me. Timing is important — Johnny Carson has a throw pillow in his house that has embroidered on it, "It's All in the Timing."

I earn my living in comedy, but science is my hobby. I'm a fan of science: I hang out with scientists at science places and I read about science and scientists. My mom always says, "If you walk like a duck, talk like a duck, and hang around with ducks, people will start thinking you're a duck." This may be true for juvenile delinquents and waterfowl, but, unfortunately, if you walk like a scientist, talk like a scientist, and hang around with scientists, people will still know you're a dumb-assed comedian.

Because some scientists like to hang out with dumb-assed comedians, they let me watch space shuttle launches from the V.I.P. viewing area. That area is 3.7 miles from the pad. Three point seven miles is a very long way to throw a house cat (you'd need some apparatus), but it's pretty stinkin' close to watch human beings get blasted into space. If you know anyone who knows anyone who knows anyone (we can get several degrees past Will Smith and Stockard Channing) who can get you V.I.P. passes to a shuttle launch, beg, call in the favor, grant sexual favors you don't enjoy — do anything, just get yourself a pass.

If you can't get a V.I.P. pass, don't beat yourself up, just go to a public viewing area. It's almost as good. You still need a pass, but you just have to ask the day before. You don't *have* to give sexual favors to anyone (but it never hurts). Even from the public areas five miles away, it is still, quite simply and without any exaggeration, the best thing you will ever see. The first shuttle launch I saw was from a way public area. We didn't even have a pass to get to the "Space Port" (what a cheesy name; I wish Disney didn't bleed into our *entire* culture). We watched it with all the RVs.

The first launch I saw was the last launch before *Challenger* blew up and, after *Challenger* blew up, everyone said that we had all been taking space launches for granted. Not me, must have been some other mother, but no, no, child, it wasn't me. Maybe TV fools took them for granted, but no one that ever stood and felt NASA explode human beings into space took them for granted. I don't ever want to have a hot beverage with anyone who would take that for granted. They wouldn't be fun.

Every morning we'd be up at 3:30 a.m., eat our traditional astronaut breakfast of steak and eggs, and sit in the car in the pouring rain like we were making out listening to the radio. It was raining the whole week of our first shuttle, and my team of space fans would get up every morning at 5 a.m. in the rain and sit in our car, dead tired, listening to the "voice of NASA," waiting for the mission to be scrubbed. We knew it would be scrubbed when we saw the rain coming down in sheets, but our motto was, "If the astronauts are getting up, we're getting up."

Finally, after several days of getting up after not going to sleep, eating donuts in the car for three hours, and then driving back to a dive hotel with nothing to do but speculate on the chances of the launch going up in the next window, it was a perfect morning. We were there in our rental car among all the RVs. Our area was all retired people in RVs with "Good Sam" stickers. Some of these people were pros: they had seen a couple Saturn IIIs. Having seen an *Apollo* mission go up is the space brag equivalent of having seen the Velvet Underground live in '67. We were neophytes and we didn't really fit in. We weren't even "Good Sams."

When it got close to going, we all got out of our vehicles. The Sams were wary of us. We were relatively young, we had leather jackets and sunglasses, and we were making loud jokes. The Sams had seen launches before, they understood things we didn't. They knew that it wasn't a time to be joking. That's the weird thing about NASA's Successful Quantifying of Comedy Timing — NASA isn't really in the comedy business.

The countdown gets close. We get down into double digits. It's dawn and you can see the shuttle artificially lit, glowing brilliantly five miles away. Mankind's lights are kicking dawn's ass in the candlepower department, and NASA hasn't really started yet. The countdown gets to single digits, and you can see the engine start. They're on their way to space. The old guy in Bermuda shorts next to me was ready; he had his handkerchief out. None of us punks were ready. The emotions caught us by surprise, we had our sunglasses in our hands and tears pouring all over our faces. Three loves-of-my-life have left me because I wouldn't cry over them the way I cried over that first space shuttle. Good Sam had his handkerchief all ready, but we had to improvise. All we could do was unzip our leather jackets, untuck our T-shirts, and pull them up to our faces. Then the P.A. system says, "Welcome to space," and I wished I'd brought another T-shirt because the one I had on was soaked with tears of awe. They were orbiting before we got back to our car. They went from five G's to weightless in the time it took me to stop sobbing.

I know, I know, I know — you've seen pictures of shuttle launches in the paper, and you've seen them on TV, and you saw *Apollo 13* and that was the bigger rocket, the VU live Saturn 5, and Opie did such a great job, you couldn't tell it was digital. Maybe you even saw the Imax movie, *The Dream Is Alive*. What a great movie, with Pinky, Ox, and Sally Ride, the sexiest woman that ever lived. In her tight blue shorts, that hair, those brains, that T-shirt, no bra, and no gravity. Goddamn me. Help me. Mr. Lee, you can keep Pamela Anderson, give me Dr. Sally to ride. Even if you've seen all that and you think you know majesty, accomplishment, and the wonder that *is* technology and humanity. Bullfeathers! You think you know that from TV? Huh? Well, don't make me laugh, I have chapped lips. When you see a shuttle go up and you see it live, make sure you bring a very big hanky. Your eyes are going to be squirting. You're going to be a big, screaming, little crybaby.

I turned into the shuttle junkie. I've been to every launch I was able to make, and that isn't enough. Thankfully, I wasn't able to make it down to the *Challenger* launch and I don't watch TV. I won't even try to imagine what it must have felt like to have that level of joy smash head on into that depth of tragedy. I feel sorry for anyone who saw that, and as far as the NASA people and the families — I can't even think about that much pain. There was nothing good about the *Challenger* disaster, but it did happen on the day that L. Ron Hubbard died and it blew that useless, evil, rat bastard's obituary off the front page and that, at least, wasn't bad.

Please don't forget, we're talking about comedy timing. I finagled my way onto Rockwell's V.I.P. bus for my next few shuttle launches. My first Rockwell party before a launch, I thought I had been around. I'd seen a few launches, I'd hung with the Good Sams. I had seen a few go up. I was chatting. I was asking people, "Have *you* ever seen a night launch before?"

One guy answered, "Not from the outside, no."

You have to be careful about trying to be cool at a Rockwell party.

Apologists try to justify spending government money on NASA by talking about all the spin-offs. I think government needs to use tax money for "police, courts, and defense" and that's it. If I were king of the world, there wouldn't be a king of the world and NASA would be private. But who cares what I think? We have NASA and they do the coolest things. It can't be justified with Tang and Crazy Glue. Exploration of space is worth it because humans need to explore. Knowledge is always good, and it's a really cool thing to see. Talk about bang for the buck. But, if you need another spin-off, well, NASA was able to quantify comedy timing.

When you see the shuttle from the V.I.P. viewing area you're looking over a wild pond/swamp, with wild pond/swamp life, 'gators and eagles and everything. Around the loudspeaker counting down, you hear nothing but the Florida swamp equivalent of crickets (which, for all I know, is crickets). It's quiet and peaceful out over the swamp/pond. "4, 3, 2, 1," and you see more smoke than you've ever seen before — clouds of heavenly, thick, white smoke.

It's nothing like bad magic show smoke. It's virgin white, technological smoke, and in the center is the light of the engines and they are burning bright.

Lou Reed went to the shuttle launch with me. See? See? Huh? — it *is* cool, the Rock and Roll Animal went. Even Debbie Harry went to see one. Ms. Harry has never done anything geeky in her life. So, see, it's not just nerd geeks and losers like me that love the shuttle — real cool people like it, too! I told Lou that we were going to see real White Light/White Heat and we did. It's 3.7 miles away and you're looking at this flame and the flame is far away and it's brighter than watching an arc welder from across a room (P&T do *not* recommend that you watch welding, but you know what we mean). It's bright. The fluffy smoke clouds of the angels of exploration spill out of your field of vision. They spill out of your peripheral vision. We're getting to where the comedy comes in.

You're 3.7 miles away, watching this controlled explosion in a rocket with human beings on top. It's the biggest explosion you've ever seen, but you're hearing . . . swamp sounds. Strain your ears, but that's all you hear — swamp crickets. People are weeping softly around you and Mission Control is saying what it needs to say, but in between you're hearing peaceful swamp. You have time to notice the quiet, wrinkle one eyebrow, and *think* to yourself, (I had one friend who actually said it out loud, but *everyone* at least thinks it), "Hmm, it seems so bright and smoky — you know, I would have thought there would be some noise."

Right as you say the word "noise" in your head, right as those synapses connect, you get hit in the chest. You don't exactly hear it at first, it almost knocks you over. It's the loudest most wonderful sound you've ever heard. Megadeth's double bass drum Quaalude thunder sounds like the Preservation Hall Jazz Band's tasteful twenty-two-incher next to this. You can't really hear it. It's too loud to hear. It's wonderful, deep and low. It's the bottom. For a bass player or a drummer nothing could give more joy. It's a squealy lead guitar player's worst nightmare. Pete Townshend said that music should be loud enough that you can't think of anything else, but it took an explosion to make him deaf. This is a real explosion and it's controlled and it's doing nothing but good and it makes your unbuttoned shirt flap around your arms. It's beyond sound, it's wind. It's a man-made hurricane. It's a baseball bat in the chest. It's so loud. It's so loud you can't even call it loud. You start cheering. You start yelling. You start crying. You are yelling from the depth of your little lizard brain. You're yelling because stinkin' animals have done this. You know the alligators are cheering and the birds and the Good Sams and every living thing on the planet is cheering. We're all cheering together because Earth animals are going into space. You can feel your throat getting raw, but you can't hear yourself scream because the shuttle is so stinkin' goddamn loud. The ground shakes and it's loud. Warfare could be louder, but this is the loudest totally good thing you will ever hear. The loudest good thing you will ever feel.

Get it? The last thing you thought was, "Hmm, it seems so bright and smoky — you know, I would have thought there would be some noise," and then there's the biggest noise, a synthetic Big-Bang-Birth-of-the-Universe noise. And the timing on the biggest noise is perfect. It is perfect comedy timing. We can measure it.

The NASA definition of comedy timing is "the difference between the speed of light and the speed of sound over a distance of 3.7 miles." The speed of light is 186,000 miles per second (I knew that off the top of my head). The speed of sound is 1,116 feet per second (I had to look that up). With the two traveling over 3.7 miles that's 17.505 seconds.

And that, my friends, is comedy timing.

THE NECKCRACKER

THERE WAS A WONDERFUL SIDESHOW mistress of ceremonies, Dolly Reagan, known on the circuit as "Dolly: Half Lady — Half Baby." Dolly had a normal woman's torso with child-size arms and legs. She was once interviewed by Tom Snyder, the late-night chat-show host, who has a talent for framing the blunt questions the rest of us rarely have the guts to ask.

Dolly's beautiful answer haunted me, and I've quoted her hundreds of times. Now, when you tell a story, it gradually changes — it may get shorter or longer or better or worse, and by the 101st time you've told it, it's never the story you started with. So, Dolly, please forgive me. This is what I learned from you, even if you never exactly said it.

Snyder's question: "How has it been, all these years, being so different from everybody else?"

Dolly smiled puckishly. "Well, I'll tell you," she said, "I was raised in a dinky little town in Canada. I was

just a young woman when the carnival came to my town. The man in the 10-in-1 show called me over and said, 'Young lady, we could use you on this show.'

"Now, at first my parents were hesitant, but the carnival man promised that if I turned out to be unhappy, he'd pay my way home, and I promised I'd always let them know where I was and how I was doing. They were good people. They understood and said yes.

"That was thirty-five years ago, and since that day I've crossed this great continent from ocean to ocean a dozen times. I've seen the most interesting places and met the most exciting people. I've earned an excellent living and brought wholesome entertainment to three generations. To top it all, I happened to find myself a fine husband and was blessed with beautiful children.

"And the people I grew up with are all still stuck in that dinky little town in Canada.

"So what I say is: Whatever you are — capitalize on it.

"Look at yourself, Tom. You're exploited for your looks, your voice, your personality. Not much difference between us . . . " here she smiled sweetly, ". . . except that I don't have to work quite so hard."

That's what I think you said, Dolly. An inconvenience in the "real" world can be money in a showbizzer's pocket. I think of Danny DeVito's height, Elton John's glasses, Patrick Stewart's slick head, Greta Garbo's accent, Don Knotts's Adam's apple.

So how do we apply this concept to travel?

When you are on a plane, your beverage is generally served in a squat, brittle plastic cup. They're not nice to drink out of, and when you're done and want to slip them into the seat pocket in front of you, they have a nasty habit of cracking and leaking ice onto your feet.

How can you turn this real-life inconvenience into exciting show business? How can you capitalize on it?

Well, imagine the plane is landing. You shake your head as though you're having trouble clearing your ears. With one hand you grasp your chin, with the other the back of your head, and appear to give your head a quick twist.

Cup here

Crush the cup

Your seatmate hears a loud, hideous cracking sound, as if you've just ruptured all seven of your cervical vertebrae. You sigh, relieved, and settle back for the landing with a smile.

It's so easy, and so shocking.

When the flight attendant asks for a beverage, order water without ice. Drink it, then wipe out the cup with your napkin. Wait for the appropriate moment, then stick your cup under your armpit. Put your hands like this and *pretend* to twist. Note we say *pretend*. See how in the photo our model is *not actually holding on to his head*? Do likewise. We are not responsible for any muttonhead who forgets he's doing a trick and breaks his own neck for a joke.

As you do your fake twist, simultaneously crush the cup under your arm.

We enjoy discovering and planning stunts that make your life zestier. But in our day-to-day life, we find people already suspect our every move, so it's hard to surprise them. This trick is an exception. We've not only done it on planes, but anywhere we find one of those unpleasant cups. (It's good practice. Sooner or later some federal agency is bound to outlaw rigid plastic cups on planes, lest anyone bruise his lips during a crash.)

We've done this trick for our eighty-year-old parents and they reached

for their nitro pills. Teller was once auditioning for the role of a suicidal Shakespearian actor. He snuck his own cup into the audition room and got the part. Directors don't forget you when you make them jump out of their thick skins.

And don't stop here. The world is full of problems. Capitalize.

Do this trick only if you are wearing long sleeves. Avoid tank-tops and sleeveless evening gowns. Make sure there is plenty of cushioning under your arm to keep you from cutting yourself with the shards of sharp plastic.

COMMITMENT PROBLEMS?
HOW ABOUT A TATTOO OF BLOOD?
A Scam for the One You Love

"You got tattoos of crosses
you got tattoos of saints
tattoos that are
and some tattoos that ain't
tattoos of Harleys
on butts covered with crud
But one thing you ain't got
is a tattoo of blood

Tattoo of Blood
Tattoo of Blood
One thing you ain't got is a Tattoo of Blood"

— LOU REED

PEOPLE ARE GETTING TATTOOS LIKE THEY'RE going out of style, and they are. When someone tells me they're thinking about a tattoo, I tell them to get a primary or secondary sexual characteristic pierced. It's cooler, it's sexier, and — when you don't like it anymore — lose the metal, let it heal, and you're done. Of course, a piercing isn't a tattoo. It's a different thing.

I understand the fascination with tattoos. Our road crew is the greatest group of human beings ever assembled and our "tattooed, hippie, redneck, biker, light man," Stewart Wagner, is a giant among giants. He's tattooed all over. Most cities we play, Stewart stops into the local shop and "gets some ink." It's a committed version of the "I Climbed Mt. Washington" stickers all over Winnebagos. Anywhere — backstage or at strip bars — he's always stripping off his pants to show someone something drawn on him, whether anyone wants to see it or not. Stewart is a very open and sharing person. Even with his clothes on, everyone knows Stewart is tattooed. You can see his arms, his hands, and his neck (he has the Japanese characters for "red" and "neck" on his neck . . . in red). There's no turning back for Stewart. He takes longer to get through airport security than I do. He even has two Penn & Teller tattoos. Loyalty.

Penn & Teller's Lighting Designer
— Stewart Wagner.

I had always wanted to get a temporary tattoo. Most people think of a temporary tattoo as a decal that is put on with water and stays for a few days or maybe even a week (depending on hygiene).

Okay, so that is a temporary tattoo, but that misses too much of the tattoo experience for my taste. With a decal tattoo, all you experience is the art and, maybe for some, the identification with those who really have tattoos (a tattoo used to mean you were a sailor, carny, or biker; now it means you're a kid who goes to a mall).

You also miss all the decision making and self-examination (for

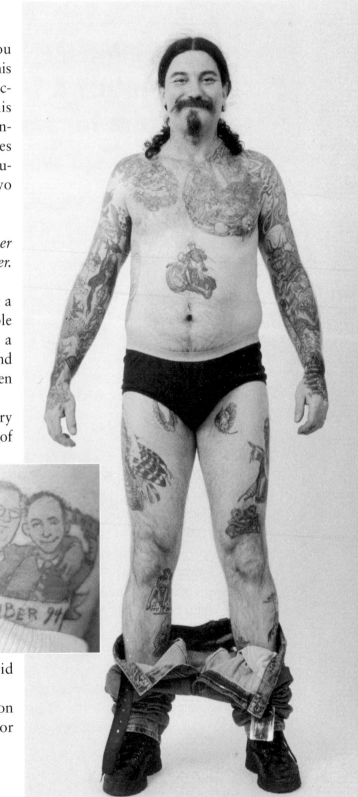

those who are sober for the tattooing process) that goes with making a lifelong decision. You also miss the pain (again, for those who are sober). To have a tattoo, you make the decision to have a needle stuck into your skin about an eighth of an inch deep many, many times. An eighth of an inch isn't very deep, but it's deep enough to get those pain receptors saying "howdy." On new tattoos, the swelling and blood of the repeatedly pierced skin overwhelms the inks that are used. I've always thought that the tattoos shown in the flash books (the loose-leaf notebooks at tattoo parlors with plastic pages of snapshots that you browse through looking for sexy inked body parts while you're checking out the work) were wonderful. The skin looks really beat up. It doesn't look like the proud owner is displaying art; it looks like forensics shots of an art attack victim. So, there are at least two questions that people with decals haven't addressed:

1. *How did you decide to modify your body permanently?*

2. *How much did it hurt?*

I've wrestled with question #1 and I can't make a decision. They can be removed, but unless you're as rich as Johnny Depp, you're probably going to have to just cover up "Winona" with a black iron cross tat or a lot of Band-Aid brand adhesive strips. I like the commitment, I like saying to the world that my body is mine and doesn't belong to nature, a god, or a government (tattooing is still illegal in places). But I don't trust fashion. What would happen if I went out and got the perfect tattoo on my arm and three years later Jon Bon Jovi and Joe Piscopo had a copy of it on their arms? There have been many bandwagons that I was riding happily until the wrong people boarded.

Even if the wrong people didn't cop my art, maybe I wouldn't like the art in a while — maybe I would become morally opposed to the art — hey, I've been wrong before (I didn't *really* believe Clinton could be that much worse than Dole). Those are the real reasons, but I have a cop-out reason as well: I'm in showbiz and maybe someday I'll want to act (I've had parts before, but it didn't look like I wanted to act). I wouldn't want to have to cover up a tattoo with makeup every day. (Goodness, is that a lame reason?! Sean Connery covered up his tattoo

for James Bond and he did okay. I should just stick with the Bon Jovi/Pis-copo reason.)

Question #2 really interests me. I like the idea of deciding some-thing is going to hurt and doing it to find out how much. I don't like accidents much, and I hate illness, but I enjoyed having a tiny amount of dental work done to see what it was like without Novocaine. It was nice to know a little of the real deal. I always think being in pain for glory is a fun thing. Pain without injury fascinates me. Pain without fear is just another sensation. I could go on, but you already know too much about me.

In 1993 I visited lovely Milwaukee (this *is* a travel book). I was cov-ering the 90th anniversary party for Harley Davidson in Milwaukee for Showtime. Bobcat Goldthwait, Paul Provenza, Richard Belzer, Stephanie Hodge, Judy Tenuda, and I were walking around the grounds with cam-era crews, making fun of bikers while making sure that it was very clear to the bikers that we weren't making fun of them. I told Jerry, the pro-ducer, that I should get a tattoo on camera but I didn't want anything per-manent. Provenz' had worn a fake nose-ring for one shot and the crew were all wearing decals and that wasn't what I wanted. I told him I want-ed a tattoo done with needle but without ink. All the pain of a tattoo but nothing to show for it. Jerry liked the idea. He went to a tattoo trailer to set it up. He came back and said it was a done deal, they would do the tattoo with blood red ink but no needle, it would look like I was being tattooed but I wouldn't be. With no needle, the red ink would wipe right off.

"That's not what I want, Jerry. I want a *needle* and no *ink*, that'll work too, won't it?" Jerry checked, and the guy said that a "dry needle" would hurt a bit more than a regular tattoo but it wouldn't leave a mark for more than several weeks. I heal quickly (one of my best character traits), so I was ready.

We got a few cameras and I went over to talk to the tattoo artist, Bubba. I talked to him before we went on camera and then asked him the same questions on camera: Yes, he used clean needles. Yes, it would hurt more without the ink to lubricate. Yes, it would bleed more without the ink to coagulate. After a couple genital jokes, he told me the forearm and the chest hurt the most. I wanted it to show often, and I have an attrac-tive forearm so I'd use the right forearm. I told him I wanted it all freehand, no stencil. I didn't want the stencil ink to get into the wound and give me an accidental half-assed tattoo.

A crowd was gathering and the cameras were rolling. He brought the needle out of the little sealed packet, and Bubba (did I mention his name was Bubba?) got to work. He asked me what I wanted. I said it didn't matter. He asked me if I liked skulls.

Who doesn't like skulls? It would be a freehand skull. Bobcat stood behind him as he brought down the needle, and gave a Bobcat scream to startle him at the moment of contact. Bobcat had to make jokes, I was just staring at the needle. The needle went in, it went in many times. The bikers were impressed, not that I was taking the pain, but that I was taking the pain for no reason. All the pain and none of the gain — they got it. I asked Bubba if it would hurt less if I loosened up my muscle and he said yes. Of course I couldn't loosen the muscle, it hurt too much. I tightened the muscle, I'm a nut. The blood was flowing. It was art being made of my blood. I watched and I liked it. The crowd was yelling that I was crazy. Having that collection of pots call me black was one of the prouder moments in this kettle's life.

How much did it hurt? That's the question I wanted to answer.

It hurt about as much as putting a couple cigarettes out on my skin (don't ask). It was a burn. But it was pain without injury, pain without fear. It was a good hurt. It didn't take long, a line-drawn skull about the size of a quarter. It looked like it was drawn in red ink, but it was my blood. It was running down my arm and doing a nice job for the camera. The bit should have been over, but Bobcat thought I should have cross-bones. He also thought I should have the full skeletal system, a Harley, and a road going up over my shoulders with lush scenery, but I was done after the crossbones. It wasn't Bubba's best work. Another artist said it was "strictly jailhouse," but Bubba was working without a stencil and there was the pressure of a crowd and TV.

I wouldn't let him put a bandage on it. I wanted the opportunity to show it off and talk about it. I had to put Neosporin on it for about a week. After about seven hours, it was at its best — the blood had started to change color and the head of the skull was the color of flesh around day-old stitches.

They said it would be gone in about five weeks, but it took about a year and a half. (How many dermatological specialists named Bubba do you know?) Lou Reed thought it was so cool that he wrote a song about it, and my band, The Captain Howdy, recorded it. I would like you to read the first part of that last sentence again: Lou Reed thought it was so cool that he wrote a song about it. Just in case the above sentence wasn't clear enough: I did something that Lou Reed thought was cool. In case you're just skimming this: *Lou Reed thought that Penn Jillette did something cool!* I got very used to the little white scar-skull on my arm. I was kind of hoping there'd be a little bit of a scar there to remind me of the needle. I was close to reinventing the tattoo.

In the past century, we have doubled life expectancy. It used to make a lot of sense to marry a teenage sweetheart, have kids fast, suffer, and die. Now, we live a way long time and it's going to keep getting longer. If you marry a teenage sweetheart now, you should be planning on a seventy-year commitment. My parents have been married over sixty-five years as I write this. That is so romantic and cool, but — hey, that's a long time. Skimming the actuary tables, planning on science improving health as it always has, and not intending to take up Ultimate Fighting, I'm still almost halfway through my life. I've had significant others. I've never been married (it's hard for an atheist from New England — no god and none of your goddamn business), but I bought a damn house with a woman — so I've been serious. Just not that serious.

My brother from a different father and mother, Tony Fitzpatrick, has his wife and kids' names tattooed on his arm. Man, how boss is that? I love seeing the ink living in his flesh like that family lives in his heart. It's a beautiful thing. But I don't have kids. I haven't *really* made a commitment to spend the rest of my life with anyone (okay, I've been doing goofy projects with this Teller guy for over twenty-three years and there's no end in sight, but — if you think I'd even write that creep's name in thin-line felt-tip on the bottom of my foot — you got another think coming). I'm not good at commitment,

Love sometimes looks like this.

but I love the painful sexiness of a loved one's name going on my arm. You get where this is going?

I have this girlfriend. I've been with her over a year. My average is three years (I used to practice serial monogamy, now I practice parallel monogamy, more efficient data transfer). I'm not sure I can commit to forty years, but, hey, a year and a half and a big hunk for the book? That I can do.

Here's a trick you can do at your hometown tattoo parlor. If you want to declare your love and

This is going to be for you, baby.

If you're lucky, you'll find a tattoo parlor half this cool.

get lots of romantic relationship points, but you might want to rethink this "lifelong" commitment every year and a half or so — here's the thing for you. Here's a way to declare very intense but still essentially temporary love — a tattoo of blood. I'm writing this so I *have* to cop to the temporary part, but when you do it you just say, "I want your name in a tattoo of blood — I want to be scarred with your name, my love." You don't have to mention the part about it going away in a year or two.

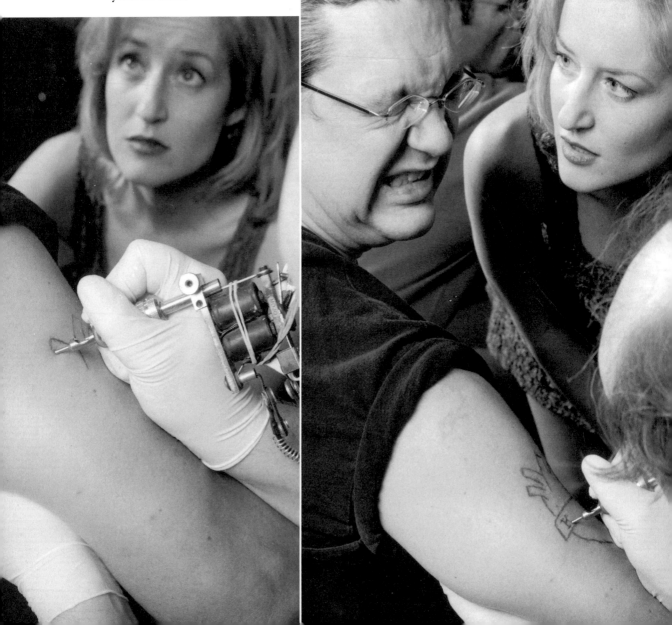

Make sure you bring your significant him or her to the parlor with you. Set it up in advance alone, so your personal Bubba understands — *no ink* — *no stencil* — just freehand needlework. Then bring your (temporary) loved one with you. You want him or her to see the blood, see the pain, see the commitment. Think about it, it's going to be a very good night after that kind of (temporary) commitment. You will be well laid.

Tony is a no-kidding artist. I called him up and asked him to do a way painful tattoo of blood with the name "Kari" in it. Stewart set us up with Mo at Las Vegas Tattoo.

Mo let Tony use his gun. Tony doesn't do tattoos. The last ones he did were with a sewing needle and India ink (you don't need to know where he did these tattoos). Tony does etching, he has a steady hand, and I trust him.

Look at the pictures. Look how impressed she was, and she knew it was temporary. *You* can pass it off as forever! Are you going to have fun the night after that blood tattoo? What do you think? You are *such* a scumball.

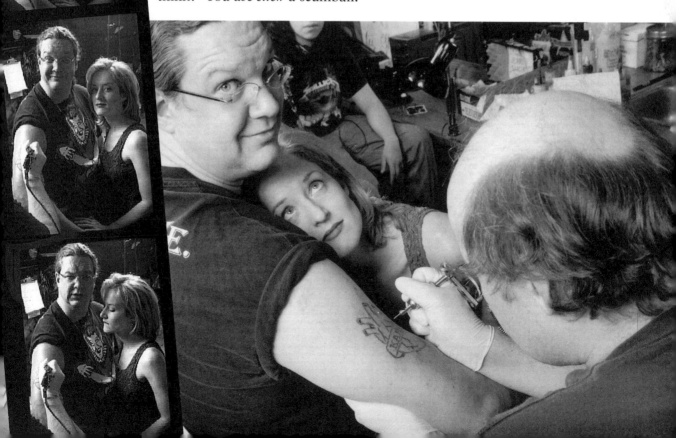

122

You can't get this with flowers and chocolates. This takes pain!

There're two things that need to be added. First of all (man, I don't like to think about this), maybe you don't have a loved one. Maybe you read our books, and like us, but there's no one that you can even commit a couple years to. Well . . . here goes: It *would* make a damn good card trick (I can't believe I'm writing this). Learn the card force on pages 5–7 and get a tattoo of blood of the card you want to force (this is so sick). I would suggest the Three of Clubs (we like that card), but, since you're not using ink and it's going to be kind of red for a while, you might want to pick a red card. How about the Three of Hearts? Hey, it would be a great trick. Rip open your shirt and say, "Is this your card?" Stewart Wagner of the P&T crew has a three of clubs ink-tattooed on his palm and he gets it *redone* when it fades (it's hard to keep a tattoo on the palm). It's a fine trick.

Is this your card?

Second, and most important, as far as I know, this tattoo of blood thing has only been done twice and both times by me. Someone told me after a show about someone they knew who did it and someone else called a radio show to say they did it, but — you know, we have some nuts get in touch with us and some of them lie. All I know about for sure is me. I don't know about you. Maybe without the ink, you'll get blood poisoning and have your arm swell up like a water condom at a frat party, rot, and fall off. Maybe you don't heal as well as I. Maybe you'll have "Foxy Mama Becky" carved in sickly white on your body for the rest of your embarrassed life. I don't know much about this. If you do it and it doesn't work out, don't blame me. As a matter of fact, this whole few pages is just a joke — it's a comedy piece — no one is supposed to really do it. Is that clear enough?

IT'S SAFE. IT'S VERY VERY SAFE.
A Mean Trick Dedicated to Krasher

THIS IS A MEAN TRICK. IT'S AN EASY TRICK. It's a fun trick. It's a real good laugh. (We're being redundant; we said it was a mean trick.)

Krasher works with Penn & Teller. Krasher is not his real name. He has a real name that sounds too much like "Penn," and we hate confusion unless we're creating it, so his name changed. He's more than earned the name Krasher.

Krasher used to be afraid to fly. If you so much as said the word "crash," his face would turn red and his hands would turn white. If you sat behind him during takeoff and kicked his seat, he would yell. Flying with the Krash Man was a Technicolor/sound extravaganza. We tortured him and he got better. He's fine now. We have named this trick to honor Krasher having his irrational fear humiliated out of him. This airplane trick would have put the pre-P&T Krasher in the nut house. This is a mean trick.

Why would you want to do a mean trick to someone whose only sin is being afraid to fly? Because being afraid to fly is stupid. Being afraid to fly hurts people. How does it hurt people? We'll tell you. It hurts people because every time one of these Luddites lips off about their fear of flying they spread the evil meme of airplane fear like a virus and other weak people decide not to fly. These nonflyers don't just stay home. When they decide not to fly, they drive. Mile for mile, the more people drive instead of fly, the more people die in auto accidents. Statistically it has to be that some of that horrible twisted highway wreckage was actually *caused* by people who should have been flying. Maybe one of these chicken-liver-green-guts-should-be-flyers hit a kid, maybe a busload of kids. Maybe a busload of quiet well-behaved kids that would have gotten together and discovered a cure for some awful disease when they grew up.

These are the kinds of things you're going to have to think about to do this trick. This is a mean trick.

Maybe it's easier than that, maybe you just hate the "friend" that you're going to pull this on. That's fine, too. You might even be nutty enough to do this to a stranger. If you are — please don't ever come near us and don't leave our books lying around your house. If you leave this book lying around, make sure you underline this next sentence: It's a very mean trick. We're not pretending this is good clean fun.

Your typical airplane safety card is designed to humor people like the irrational coward Krasher used to be. The card daintily omits any reference to suffocation, even as it tells you what to do when there's no oxygen to breathe. Without a word about drowning, it tells you how to inflate a life vest and a raft, and how to use your seat cushion for flotation on the cold, black sea. The card shows you brace-positions and thoroughly briefs you on what to do if you see smoke, fire, and debris, but avoids the term "crash" as though, by some atavistic logic, if we avoid the word, we make the thing itself disappear.

This makes it the perfect prop for alarming aerophobes.

Imagine you are on an airplane, looking over the safety card and chatting with your seatmate. "I guess," you say, taking out the safety card, "they tell you to read these cards before the plane takes off, because if you *crash* there wouldn't be time to read them then. I guess in a *crash*, heck, maybe the lights would go out, maybe there'd be smoke and flames in your face, which would slow down your reading."

You take out the airline magazine and turn to the map of plane routes. "Gee," you say, "I wonder where planes *crash* the most. Wait, let's try a game. Let's imagine we're *crashing* in Europe. Here, you pick a city. No, wait. Don't look. Let's pick one at random."

Now at this point you may be done. Your seatmate may be throwing up from the psychological assault. Or she/he may have changed seats. But if your seatmate is still present and conscious, you proceed as follows:

You hand your seatmate a ballpoint pen. "Now," you say, "hold the map facedown and put the pen underneath. Make a little dot somewhere on Europe." Your seatmate (hoping that if he/she cooperates you will eventually shut up) obliges and you take back the pen. When you turn the map face up, you see this:

"Wow, cool! Paris!" you exclaim. "Maybe we'll get

impaled on the Eiffel Tower — *n'est-ce pas?* Gee, I wonder if the safety card can tell us what to do ... "

You open the safety card. There, apparently *printed* on the card is this: ▶

Please don beret before crashing in France

Now, this may be the magic moment. Your pantywaist co-flyer may laugh. This psychological dam may break, and he/she may be purged of irrational fear. You will have the satisfaction of changing somebody's life.

Or this may be the last straw. The apparent fact that a randomly imagined crash is already listed on the safety card may push your victim over the edge and result in spontaneous weeping. You have the satisfaction of seeing justice done.

But now comes the afterkick:

"Excuse me," you say, "but I'm going to go comb my hair. Wouldn't want to look unkempt if we *crash*." You get up and go to the washroom. You leave the safety card behind, temptingly. Your seatmate compulsively grabs for it to confirm that he/she is not going nuts.

The message and the drawing of the beret have vanished. Gone. Your seatmate is now sure he/she's having a breakdown. Your satisfaction is complete.

To pull off this hallucinogenic swindle, you need three things. The first is a pen that doesn't really write. It's just a dried-up ball-point pen, and if you want to know how to make one quickly, look on pages 162–163.

The second is a little clear acetate flap that looks exactly like the picture of the beret on the previous page. We've bound one into this book. Turn to page 132. The facing page is clear acetate, printed for the trick. Cut it out *very* carefully so that the cut edge matches right up with the outside edge of the frame.

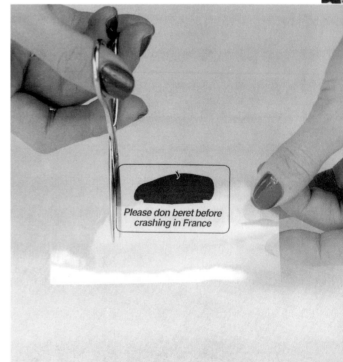

Please don beret before
crashing in France

The third is a real ballpoint pen.

Carry these tools whenever you fly. You might want to wrap the acetate and keep it in your wallet. Before you get your seatmate's attention, moisten the back of the acetate with water (if available) or spit (always handy) and press it tightly against the glossy surface of the safety card wherever you find a plausible empty spot for it.

Then while your seatmate is busy biting fingernails, take out the airline magazine, and with the *working* ballpoint pen, make a little dot over Paris.

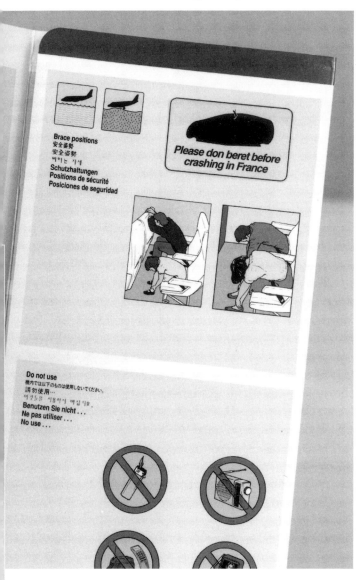

With all your homework done, lead the conversation as we have described. When the time comes, offer the dried-up pen, turn the magazine so the map is facing down, and guide your seatmate's hand into the general area of Europe. You don't want the victim "making the dot" way down in Madagascar and later finding it at the other end of the map page. If you keep your seatmate's pen point in the vicinity of Europe, you're completely covered.

Take back the pen and show the map, pointing out that your seatmate "chose" Paris. Take out the safety card, and appear amazed to discover that the airline has been so foresightful as to include directions for impromptu Gallic landings.

Now for the kicker. Excuse yourself to comb your

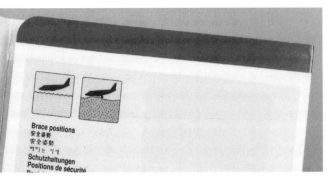

hair. As you get up, sneak the acetate piece off the safety card, and gently wipe any telltale moisture off the surface. Drop the card casually on your seat while you go to the rest room, where you clean and repack your acetate gimmick in your wallet.

Had enough of crashing in France? Why not try Holland?

In the event of a water landing in the Netherlands, wooden shoes may be used for flotation.

YOUR GUARDIAN-VARIETY VEGETABLE

T WO HUNDRED YEARS AGO, YOU COULDN'T use a picture to prove jack. There were no photographs and it was just too damn easy to draw things different than they really appeared in the world. Photography came along and for a while the camera didn't lie, at least not easily. Now that the world is digital, it's trivial for the camera to lie and it lies well. We have to go back to getting the truth from people. That's okay, that's the only place truth ever lives.

We all know that regular cameras lie with darkroom tricks, and digital cameras lie with a click, point, and boom, my head's on a Fabio-like body.

Pictures lie.

But a Polaroid still feels pretty trustworthy. Pretty WYSIWYG. If it shows up on a Polaroid, it was there. Wanna bet? Not for you. Not anymore. Not now that you have this book.

It wouldn't be a Penn & Teller book without gimcracks, and we got one of the coolest ever bound right into the book. Facing page 132 there is a sheet of acetate and on that sheet of acetate are little pictures. We're going to tell you how to get those little pictures to appear mysteriously on Polaroid photographs.

This is the best kind of trick because it takes evil scams developed by hateful cheesebag phony psychics (triple redundancy) and uses it for truth, justice, and a good-natured joke to drive a so-called friend crazy. Let's hear it for our side.

Cameras are an important part of traveling. It's been said the un-photographed trip is not worth taking, and, since traveling is often way sexy, you really should be traveling with a Polaroid. Do you really want to drop off some of your sexier photos for processing? I've seen some of the "private" collections of found-art creepy artists who develop film professionally and, well, they're wonderful, they're pure art, and they're sexy. They're very sexy, but I'm not sure you want you and your loved ones to be featured. You also don't need one copy of every picture you take of your kids automatically going to the freaks at the F.B.I. So buy a Polaroid — it's private, it develops right there, it feels like you're living in the future, and you can do this super spiffy trick.

This trick was developed by the scumballs to make "spirits" or "auras" appear on a Polaroid snapshot. They've made all sorts of images appear — how about the original Madonna, the (like a) Virgin Mary? How about a dead relative, or the even more trendy angel? As a matter of fact, any picture that can be printed on acetate can be conjured out of the ether onto Polaroid film.

The Polaroid film packet is a wonder. It's film, it's developer, and it's even home to the coolest little batteries in the world. Any true geek has already pillaged these packs to, oh, I don't know, spin the propeller on his mortar board upon receiving his (there is no need for "his/hers"; in this case it's always "his") diploma from M.I.T.

You can put a piece of acetate on top of the film pack, put the whole shebang in the camera, and the camera will take its picture right through the acetate. The acetate won't be noticed, but whatever's printed on the acetate will cast a shadow on the film. Bingo, spirits from the ether. Get it?

Trim for Spectra©

Trim for 600 film/One-Step

Trim for Spectra©

Trim for Captiva©

Trim for 600 film/One-Step

Trim for Captiva©

Trim for Captiva©

Trim for Spectra©

Trim for 600 film/One-Step

Please don beret before crashing in France

(For use on Page 128 with "It's Safe, It's Very Very Safe")

CUT HERE

In the event of a water landing in the Netherlands, wooden shoes may be used for flotation.

WHAT YOUR SUCKER WILL SEE AND BELIEVE

Mr. or Ms. Sucker will think of a vegetable. You'll take his or her picture with a perfectly ordinary, everyday, household, no-kidding Polaroid camera and the chosen vegetable will come from the great beyond and show up right in the picture with him or her. They'll just *think* of a vegetable, any vegetable! And it'll really be on the picture! Pretty amazing, huh? And wait until you see how easy it is — we even have Renée French cartoons. If you're exceptionally "cartoon literate" (hey, if people can use the phrase "visually literate" with a straight face, we can give this one a try), you might be able to do the trick without being able to read.

A REALLY EASY AND AMAZING POLAROID TRICK

UP, HERE'S ALL YOU DO.

A REALLY SMALL AMOUNT OF STUPID-EASY, SECRET, SNEAKY STUFF YOU HAVE TO DO IN ADVANCE

Cut out the "carrot" acetate to fit the size film you put in your Polaroid. Polaroids come in three basic sizes, the original square, the little-smaller-than-the-square, called the 600, and the way littler, store-the-pictures-in-the-back size. We got you covered on all three. Just cut the acetate to the size you need. We even have a little guide for you. Just cut it to the size of your film pack.

We'll start with how to use the acetate of St. Carl the Carrot for a trick.

Take a new pack of film and set the acetate on top (that's the cardboard side with the blue writing). With the acetate on top, tuck the edge right above St. Carl's cute and very righteous halo under the edge of the black plastic frame of the film pack. You're trying to get the acetate to stay in place while you slip it in. The tuck will keep St. Carl happily snug on the film pack. Carefully load the whole package — acetate and film — into the camera.

Have some paper and a writing implement somewhere handy, but *not looking like it's prepared for the trick!* Handy, but not set up.

That's it. The trick is done, the rest is just acting.

Your friend just "thinks" of a vegetable!? Well, kinda-sorta.

Start talking to your victim about guardian angels and guardian spirits. I'm guessing you'll do this *very* tongue in cheek. A survey says that around half of the people in our great country believe in angels. That may be true, but we've never met any of these well-surveyed angel-believers and we're guessing you haven't either. If you do have a friend that believes this bunk for real, well, do the trick, laugh derisively, and then get new friends. You can do better.

After you chatted up the spirit idea, state that everyone also has a "guardian vegetable." Go nuts. Talk about nutrition, just say anything that pops into your head. This is the fun part.

SCENARIO #1 — HEY, YOU MIGHT GET LUCKY

You want to memorize the next command and give it word for word. The wording is simple, but very important. Tell your victim to "Name a vegetable." It's a simple command and say it exactly that way. Don't use the word "guardian" or "favorite" at this point in the trick. Just tell him or her to name a vegetable.

The odds are in your favor that it'll be "carrot." If it's "carrot" — you got lucky — your work is done. But it's not just that your work is done. You are really set up for a miracle. It's an amazing trick anyway, but if she or he says "carrot" it's a miracle that can never be figured out. No one will ever know that you had a plan if he or she didn't say "carrot!" As far as the world is concerned, you said, "Name a vegetable," and you made that vegetable appear on a Polaroid picture. It will be the best trick anyone has ever seen. You can take that person to every Penn & Teller show that comes to your town and we'll never touch it. She or he will come out of *our* show saying, "Yeah, they're pretty good with shooting the bullets at each other and everything but, hey, they can't touch your carrot" (maybe your friend will have a wording that doesn't have that weird sexual vegetable double entendre, but that'll be the idea). And, when this does happen (and if you do the trick a few times it will; "carrot" is the most named vegetable), you are finished — skip the whole next step and go to the fun taking the picture part.

NOTE: You can go to the next section: "Here's the Miracle" on page 138, if the rube does say "carrot" right off.

SCENARIO #2 — YOU DON'T GET LUCKY AND IT'S STILL A GODDAMN MIRACLE

If the victim doesn't say "carrot," it's still a very good trick and a very easy trick. You don't have to practice this next move. As long as you understand the concept, you can do this the first time out. When she or he says a vegetable other than "carrot," take your piece of paper from the handy but not obvious spot and rip it up so you have a few pieces of paper (no one needs to think about how many) that look pretty much alike — the more alike they look, the better. Let's say the first vegetable named is "broccoli" (the next most likely after "carrot"). Pick up a piece of paper and a writing implement and repeat "broccoli" aloud, as you write on the piece of paper. *But here's the trick* — as you say "broccoli," *don't* write "broccoli," write "carrot." She or he will just assume you're writing "broccoli." As a matter of fact, you're going to find it really hard *not* to write "broccoli" as you say it. *But if you want the trick to work* write "carrot." Fold up the piece of paper and put it aside. Ask again, with careful wording, "Name another vegetable." Let's say it's "cucumber" — repeat "cucumber" aloud as you write "carrot" on a piece of paper. Get it? No matter what's said you're going to write "carrot." If someone says, "Karen Ann Quinlan," you say, "That's a very obscure and dated joke in very bad taste, but I'll write it down," and, while you're saying that, you write "carrot." You're going to keep writing "carrot" on different pieces of paper, until she or he really says "carrot" and then you're going to write "carrot" again when you hear "carrot." Eventually, he or she will say "carrot" and after that, you're going to ask her or him to name another vegetable and you're going to write "carrot" again on another piece of paper. You can stop after you get "carrot," but you don't want to stop immediately after you get "carrot," or it'll look like you were waiting for "carrot" (which you were, but

no one needs to know that). You want to do at least one more vegetable after "carrot" to make the trick better. Don't be stupid, when she or he says the vegetable after "carrot," you're going to repeat it aloud and then write "carrot." You ain't writing nothing but "carrot." No matter what, you write "carrot." Now, he or she will assume (making an ass out of her or him but not "u") that you've written a different vegetable on each of those pieces of paper, but you've really just written "carrot" over and over. Have the victim pick one at random, out of a hat or a bowl or something and look at it. Guess what. The chosen paper will say "carrot." Shut him or her up. Have the "choice" kept secret. You don't want to know. Don't look. Nobody should say "carrot" aloud until the punch line. This is such an easy way to get someone to pick "carrot" at "random," but it kills. Take all the other "carrot" papers and put them absentmindedly in your pocket.

HERE'S THE MIRACLE

Say the "choice" might be her or his "guardian vegetable." Tell him or her to concentrate on his or her "guardian vegetable." Make sure no one says the word "carrot" again. Keep saying "guardian vegetable." You want everyone to remember that he or she just thought it. You want them to remember wrong. Remembering wrong is a big part of showbiz ("DeNiro is *always* great"). Keep saying stuff like, "Whatever your vegetable was, concentrate on it." "Concentrate really

hard on the vegetable you chose." Act like you don't know which vegetable they picked.

Find a place for your victim to pose where the background is light. There needs to be a light, blank space right over the victim's left shoulder. See how St. Carl the Carrot is watching benevolently over our left shoulder? You want to leave a nice light-colored area camera for St. Carl to appear. Take a minute and look at the sample pictures. Tell your victim *exactly* how to stand to psychically project the guardian vegetable. You remember where the carrot is on the acetate, so you have an idea of where the carrot is going to be on the photo. Picture where the carrot was when you put the acetate on the film and frame your picture so St. Carl will have a nice spot to appear.

Make the victim work. Make him or her suffer. If she or he is a believer in angels, make him or her really suffer. Make sure he or she is standing just so — "a little to your left," "a little to your right," "a little towards me," "a little back" (the last command is great if she or he is on the edge of the Grand Canyon — we won't miss one believer). Wait until he or she has a really stupid expression on his or her face and snap the photo.

Polaroids take a while to develop, and that's the genius part of this trick. That'll give you time to cop the acetate. It's loud and it's awkward, so you can't do it right in front of your audience. When the picture comes out of the camera, don't touch it. Hold the camera out and let the victim take it. You've done your dirty work, you don't want anyone thinking you did something fishy while handing off the picture. When she or he takes it, peek at the non-developed picture over his or her shoulder and act really depressed that there's no picture. What kind of idiot would have a Polaroid and not know it takes the picture a little while to develop? The kind of idiot that would have a friend that's about to believe in a "guardian vegetable."

YOU HAVE SOME "ALONE TIME"
— USE IT TO CLEAN UP

Tell your victim to sit down and concentrate. You feel that maybe your strange vibe may scare and confuse the "guardian vegetable," so you will leave to allow the vegetable spirits to do their thing without interference. Before you leave the area, tell him or her to call you back when something develops. How's that for misdirecting from a magic move? You're going to *leave the room* to do your sleight of hand. Close the door, or run around the corner, get far enough away that they can't see or hear you. When you're safe in the bathroom (it's a very magical place) or wherever, open the camera and remove the acetate.

When you close the camera it's going to eject the next picture automatically (yup, you're going to waste the next picture — miracles aren't cheap). This will make a noise like, oh, like someone ejecting a picture from a Polaroid camera, that's why you have to be far away. Peel the St. Carl the Carrot's acetate off the film pack and store it in a safe, secret place. You need to get rid of the wasted picture and all the "carrot" slips that are still in your pocket. (This is only if "carrot" wasn't their first choice. If they *did* say "carrot" first thing — you're done.)

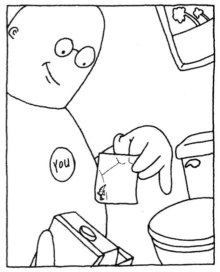

You have to get rid of the blank picture and those pesky carrot slips someplace where the victim won't check them out when thinking back on the trick. You could just leave them in your pocket and throw them away later, and that's best, but if you are going to throw them away, make sure that no one is going to check them out. Penn & Teller's absolutely favorite magical method is blowing our noses into guilty pieces of trash. That's right, blow your snot all over the blank picture and the "carrot" papers. This is the professional way. Ask anyone that knows Penn & Teller and they'll tell you that we blow our noses on anything and everything. All good professional and amateur performers should cultivate this habit. No one (except Penn & Teller) is going to dig through someone's fresh snot just to figure out how a trick is done. Remember: you *can* just leave the guilty trash in your pockets and blow your nose on it later.

With the acetate out of the camera and the guilty trash gone, run back to wait for the yell that something's happened. No one will miss you, they've been watching the photo develop (still one of the true wonders of the modern world even without a guardian carrot). You'll be ready to come back into the room with a perfectly-normal-everyday-acetate-free camera (but, you don't want to point that out.)

It's a miracle. St. Carl *was* watching over your friend — photographic proof of a guardian vegetable.

How boss is this trick? Your victim thought of a vegetable picked at random and it appeared on their picture in spirit photography. This trick will *kill kill kill!* And all you have to do is get a piece of plastic in and out of a camera and write "carrot" a lot. What could be easier?

HOW COULD IT BE ANY HARDER?

Well, glad you asked. If you're really a tightass who wants a perfect trick, or if you don't like to blow your nose in scrap paper (you're missing one of the true joys in life) you can try this: Before you start, write lots of different vegetables on pieces of paper that are just like the pieces of paper you're going to use for the trick. After they pick "carrot," put the other "carrot" slips in your pocket. While she or he is looking at the picture developing and you're in your real or figurative bathroom copping acetate, put about the right number of random vegetable papers in your pocket and throw the others away (or, if there's a chance anyone will see the trash, just leave them in a different pocket or blow your nose on them). When the picture is developed, just pull out all the pre-made, random, vegetable papers and casually leave them around. It's a very easy switch — *you're in another room.* If you want, later when you're alone, you can blow your nose on the carrot papers just for fun.

HOW ABOUT A REAL RELIGIOUS TRICK WITH NO WORK AT ALL?

Glad you asked. We also put an acetate with the (like a) Virgin Mary just floating there (scope out the face). Just slide it in the film pack and produce a miracle. No real plotted trick, just a little miracle. The tabloids will be knocking down your door. You'll have a career. What else could be easier?

WE NEVER GET ENOUGH CARD TRICKS

Glad you asked. Well, just as easy, if you already know a card force (and you do, from pages 5–7) is to force the Three of Clubs and use the Three of Clubs acetate. You should be able to figure it out from there, but just in case:

Put the right size Three of Clubs acetate on your film, tuck it in, and slide the whole shebang into the camera.

Have someone "pick" a card — use the method on page 6 to *make* them pick the Three of Clubs. If you don't like that envelope method, hey, we got two other books and they each have all sorts of ways to control someone's "totally free" choice of a card. But, we're not here to pimp our other books to you — you're fine using the envelope method.

Have the victim stand like an idiot (sometimes X = X) like she or he was waiting for St. Carl the Carrot.

Take the picture. Let her or him wait for it to develop while you leave the room to cop the acetate and, boom, the Three of Clubs is in a picture with the victim. "Is that your card?" You don't even *have* to blow your nose into the rest of the cards. (But you can if you want. We would.)

WHAT ELSE?

Well, now that you know the Penn & Teller Polaroid scam, you can draw any picture you want, right onto a piece of acetate with a Sharpie (or any kind of plain black marker — remember, it's the shadow that's making the picture — we didn't print in black on the acetate *just* to be cheap. If you think about using colors, you're just thinking stupid — maybe *you* have a guardian vegetable), cut it to the right size, and get it to appear on a Polaroid picture.

Here's an idea: with our first book, *Penn & Teller's Cruel Tricks for Dear Friends*, we packaged a book of short stories, called *Would, Could, Should*. They're nice little short stories, but the top line of every page describes an image that looks kinda sorta like this:

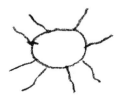

If you draw that onto an acetate and cut it to the right size you could put that image on a picture. Use *Would, Could, Should* as described in the first book to get your victim concentrating on that image "at random" (these directions aren't very hard; you just get them to open *Would, Could, Should* to any page and concentrate on the top image). If you have the right acetate in the camera, all you have to do is get the sucker to pose, snap a photo and you have a punch line that proves your camera is a mind reader. If you have access to a copier (and how many of you are reading this book deep in a rain forest?), you can make copies of our page and any of your drawings and keep them in reserve.

IT'S A GODDAMN MIRACLE

Yup, it's a goddamn miracle. You will be able to start a religion. This will be the best trick anyone you know has ever seen. It's worth cutting some acetate and lying.

Let's take a moment and silently thank Edwin Herbert Land. What a guy.

BILLET DEUCE

SOMETIMES WHEN YOU TRAVEL, YOU HAVE to go alone. Loved ones have lives and plans of their own, and those plans may not include tagging along for a fall tour of regional theatres in the Pacific Northwest. How do you keep love alive when you're miles and months apart?

You can phone (but, oh, be careful; those late-night, long-distance arguments are the worst). If you have the budget, you can send balloons and strip-o-grams. But for showing you care, nothing beats a letter. Unfortunately, writing letters on the road is harder than it sounds. It's hard to think of romantic stuff when you're jet-lagged and the food is beige and the locals talk funny.

So we offer you this: an eerie combination of love letter and card trick. It's amazing, romantic, and cheaper than a fruit basket.

You have about five minutes of homework to do before you depart on your trip (we'll tell you about this later). Then, when you leave, take a copy of the following pages. If you have pretty handwriting, copy it by hand. If not, take a photocopy and add your signature. Then, when you need that touch of *l'amour* send it by mail or fax; or even transcribe it on your laptop and send it via e-mail from your modem.

To grasp the power of the trick, we suggest you get a pack of cards, and discard the jokers and advertising cards. Then follow the directions as your sweetheart will (of course, for now, you'll have to imagine the beginning part where the pack of cards is discovered). If you do everything right, you will amaze yourself.

Darling Love o' my Life,

Tonight I missed you, oh, how I missed you! I'm jet-lagged,
the food is beige, and the locals talk funny, which makes me miss
you even more. I missed you so much that, just to distract myself,
I decided to learn a card trick from the Penn & Teller book. I
bought a pack of cards at the newsstand. Then I came back to my
digs and practiced.

When I finished practicing, I put the cards on the night table,
and fell asleep. I dreamed about you — you and the deck of cards.

In my dream I was standing in our bedroom at home with the new
pack of cards in my hand. You, my sweet patootie, were sleeping,
breathing that little-kid way you do when you're really deeply
gone. I leaned over and kissed you, and you kissed me back without
waking, then rolled over and curled up. I crept around to my side
of the bed so I wouldn't disturb you, and slipped the pack of cards
under the mattress. I could almost smell the warm, sweet bedcov-
ers.

Then suddenly I woke up. I couldn't get the dream out of my
mind and I couldn't fall back to sleep. So I thought I might as
well practice the card trick.

I turned on the light. But the deck — I was sure I had left it on the night table — was gone. I searched behind the table, in the drawer, under the bed, in my luggage. Gone! I began to wonder whether I had ever really bought a deck at all or if that was part of the dream, too.

Now, I know it sounds nutty, but would you do me a favor, honeybun? Please? Would you go look under the mattress on my side of the bed, up near the head end? It's a nutty thing to ask, I know ...

Well? Was it there? The deck I put under the mattress in my dream? It was? I knew it!

This is going to sound even nuttier, but since you have the cards — would you mind if I tried my new card trick right now? I want to feel your fingers on my pasteboards.

Are you willing to try?

Then sit on our bed.

Now sort the deck of cards into two piles; we'll call them male and female. The male pile will contain all the odd-numbered cards along with the aces, jacks, and kings (A, 3, 5, 7, 9, J, K). The female pile will contain all the even-numbered cards and the queens (2, 4, 6, 8, 10, Q).

You won't find any jokers. I just checked. They're here in my trash can. I threw them away before I went to sleep.

Now, O fire of my loins, please take the female (even) pile and shuffle the cards. While you shuffle, think back on our first kiss.

Whenever the impulse strikes you, stop shuffling and look at the top card and the bottom card. Add their values together (a queen counts as 12) and remember the total. We'll call that the secret number of our kisses. In ancient times lovers believed that as long as the number of their kisses stayed a secret, no jealous witch could hex them. So remember that number, but never, never say it aloud.

Now set down the female pile and pick up the male. Shuffle that pile, and think back on the first time we made love (I know I was a little clumsy, but I was so excited I'm surprised I didn't pass out).

Whenever you want, stop shuffling. Hold the pile facedown and count down to the card at the secret kiss-number position. For example, if the number were eighteen, you'd look at the eighteenth card from the top of the pile. Go ahead now, count down and look at the card at the kiss-number position. Don't take it out. Just look at it.

Now make a promise. Promise to remember this card forever. Then promise you will never, never say its name, not to anyone, not even to me. Like the number of our kisses, it will be an unspoken pact between us, safe in its secrecy.

Close up the pile of cards in your hands, leaving our love-card undisturbed in the same random location you found it. Hold that "male" pile facedown, and pick up the other ("female") pile and put it facedown on top.

And now for the magic: I'm going to prove to you that the same secret lives in both our hearts.

In a row, deal out one card for each of the letters in the word

KISSES

Now make sure no one is watching, then quickly deal out the
number of our kisses, laying out one card for each kiss on top of
each of the KISSES cards. When you come to the end of the KISSES
row, just start again at the beginning and keep dealing until our
kisses are all dealt.

Now, before any prying devils can count our kisses, continue
and deal out one card for each letter of

OURSECRET

and immediately sweep aside all the cards you have dealt into a
jumbled heap. Well done! Our secret is safe.

And now, to give me the power to act across the miles, spell a
message, dealing out one card for each letter of

ILOVEYOU

Oh, thank you. Here in this lonely and distant place, with
beige food and funny-talking locals, I feel your words tingling
under my skin like fire.

And now, from afar, powered by your love, I command our secret
card to come forth. I command it.

Then softly, tenderly, I say to you,

Turn up the next card.

There! Just as I told you. Our love card, the . . . no! I mustn't say it! We promised we would never speak its name. A promise is a promise. A secret is a secret. But now I know that you know that I know. So good night, dreamboat. I'm ready to sleep.

Maybe next time I'll wake up beside you.

Your love slave,

P.S. I've just noticed something strange. The jokers I saw in my trash basket not ten minutes ago are gone! I bet they overheard my thoughts (good thing I didn't say the name of our secret love-card!) and dreamed their way through space and time there to our bedroom, too.

Watch out! They could be anywhere. And those jokers are awful thieves. I bet while you were searching for our love-card, they stole something from right under your cute nose. If I know them (and I do), they hid what they stole under the mattress again — maybe this time on your side of the bed.

Why don't you go check?

THE SETUP

Before you leave on your trip, buy a pack of cards. Throw away the advertising cards and doctor the Ace of Hearts to look like the one shown. Of course use your own initials and those of your honey-bunch instead of the sample ones (unless you want to be closer to Penn & Teller than is probably good for you). Arrange the Ace of Hearts and the two jokers as shown under the mattress on your beloved's side of the bed. Then shuffle the pack of cards and slip it under the mattress on your side.

Now we're fully aware that your private life may be a bit different in tone from the letter we've written. This letter's really just a starting point. Feel free to add explicit personal endearments. And if you want to substitute your own message in place of

K I S S E S O U R S E C R E T

I L O V E Y O U

be our guest.

Just be aware that for the trick to work, you have to sum up your relationship in exactly twenty-three letters. No more. No less.

ANIMAL CUNNING

IN OUR CAREER, WE'VE PRODUCED LIVE BEES, made leeches vanish, and snipped boa constrictors in half on network television. We've dropped anvils on ducks and nowadays make rabbits disappear by popping them into chipper-shredders. But we never play with livestock on international tours. We're not just lazy (though actually we are, terribly); we've learned from friends how maddening it can be to try to get even a cockroach past customs officials.

Our favorite horrific/ingenious getting-animals-past-borders story was confided to us (so, naturally, we're making it public) by Deanna Shimada, Australian wife of Haruo Shimada, the virtuoso Japanese dove-magician. She agreed to let us tell you, but for reasons that will become apparent, maybe you should keep it to yourself . . .

The Shimadas traveled with ten doves, and performed throughout Asia for years without much difficulty at the borders. In Singapore, for example, customs inspectors are not inclined to challenge wicker luggage unless it is cooing *very* loudly. On such occasions the Shimadas used the kind of strategem that seems natural to a magician. Instead of trying to quiet the doves, they gave their toddler daughter Lisa a reed whistle. Whenever they approached inspectors, the parents asked Lisa for a little music. If the officer noticed any birdlike sounds, he credited Lisa's budding woodwind technique.

But when the Shimadas came to America to appear on the *Tonight Show* for the first time, they needed more than a whistle. U.S. customs officials instantly quarantined Shimada's doves, pending an examination by the government veterinarian. It would take place within a week, they hoped.

A week! Shimada was to appear on *Tonight* in three days. It would be his big break on American TV. He could, of course, just buy new doves, but two of his had been specially trained as the Opening Dove and the Dove on the Cane.

Shimada was torn. As a professional animal handler, he knew his birds were in perfect health. But he also knew that the bureaucracy might take too long to come to the same conclusion — maybe long enough to blow his chance on *Tonight*. When he asked Deanna's advice, she said only, "Are you a real magician, or not?"

The next afternoon, the Shimadas sat nervously in a borrowed car in the parking lot of the animal control holding station near Los Angeles International Airport. Deanna had installed four secret pockets inside the lapels of Haruo's new corduroy sport coat, and in two of those pockets were doves borrowed from a brother wizard in L.A.

The Shimadas were terrified. They hated the idea of messing with a very powerful foreign government in a country in which they would have preferred to behave as respectful guests. But the doves *were* healthy and the *Tonight Show* was so important . . . They locked the car and entered the quarantined building.

Haruo explained to the receptionist that his birds were being held under quarantine. He said they were unaccustomed to strangers and he feared they might not survive without a reassuring visit from him. Permission was granted and an officer led the Shimadas to the cage containing their ten doves.

The officer watched as Haruo picked out two of the birds (which just happened to be the Opening Dove and the Cane Dove — when you're a magician, you learn to recognize individual birds by the shapes of their heads) and examined them. "Look here," he said, pointing under the wings. "My doves have picked up parasites. Don't you have any medicine for this?"

The officer said he didn't.

"No tick powder?" Shimada asked indignantly.

The officer said, oh, yes, he might have some. He turned away for an instant to open a nearby locker.

When he turned back to report that he was out of tick powder, he saw Haruo still holding two doves. Nothing had changed, except that Deanna was now matter-of-factly brushing a few bits of white fluff off Haruo's lapel. Haruo gently released the doves into the cage, thanked the officer for trying to help, and he and Deanna headed for the car.

Once they had pulled out of the parking lot, Deanna heaved a sigh of relief and removed the Opening Dove and the Cane Dove from Haruo's secret pockets. At that instant Perry Como on the radio began crooning "It's Impossible." The Shimadas burst out laughing and laughed all the way back to their hotel.

The following day, as they were about to try and track down eight more birds to complete their cast, Haruo got a call from Customs, asking him to pick up his doves as soon as possible; the government veterinarian had certified that all the doves were healthy. The Shimadas were stunned. They had been so clever, and the authorities had *still* found a way to outwit them — by being efficient. With his feathered cast reunited, Shimada confidently launched himself in the United States with a perfect shot on the *Tonight Show*.

So the stand-in dove caper ended up being unnecessary — unnecessary to Shimada, that is. But as a tale to tell while waiting in those long lines at Customs, *we* find it absolutely indispensable.

By the way, if you happen to be an official in Customs or Immigration, this incident happened over twenty-five years ago, well outside the Statute of Limitations. And if that's not enough for you, well, then we made this story up. You know us. We lie.

This is our pal Pam Hayes, a famously funny magician's assistant. When she flies on airplanes, she stuffs her two longhaired teacup Chihuahuas into her shirt to avoid problems with airline pet restrictions (most allow only one pet per passenger). But on one occasion as she approached the security checkpoint in the airport in Frankfurt, Germany, she saw the inspectors patting down all the patrons, and she realized her dogs were too big to pass as love handles. So Pam stepped into the ladies' room, and emerged a moment later carrying this "dog." With a brazenness only a professional magician's assistant can achieve, Pam explained that the dog was a "rare Chihuahua-dachshund mix," and breezed by with a smile.

MENE MENE
TEKEL YOUFOOLEM GOOD
(the Other Killer Gideon Bible Trick)

W E WERE HIRED TO PERFORM AT probably the most exclusive Hollywood party ever. They arranged to close our Broadway show for two days and fly us to Los Angeles in a huge private jet with soft beds, a five-course meal, a library of videos for a big-screen TV, and our own personal flight attendant. We landed at a secret "executives only" airport, and were ferried by limo to a discreet little club in Beverly Hills.

There were only thirty people at the party, but these thirty people were the Who's Who of show business for that year. There were the top booking agents, the biggest box office stars, the heads of all the major studios, and the most famous director in the world. While the moguls were finding their way to their seats, host Robin Williams came backstage to report on the crowd. "Well, boys," he said with a grin, "if you bomb tonight, you don't *ever* have to worry about bombing again."

We're still in showbiz, I'm pleased to report.

Our encore was a stage-size version of this trick.

HOW IT LOOKS

You and your friend are in a hotel room where there's a notepad (look on the night table by the telephone), a ball-point pen, a bathroom mirror, and a Gideon bible. You pick up the pad, draw something on it, tear the page off, and fold it up without showing your friend what you drew. Let's imagine you drew this: ▶

You then give the pad and pen to your friend, instructing him/her to hold the pad upside down (i.e., with the writing surface facing the floor) and the pen underneath with its point touching the paper.

Now in a quiet, almost hypnotic voice, you tell your friend to move his/her hand in various ways ("Pull the pen from the paper, now put it on a different spot and draw a small squiggly line . . . " etc.). Eventually you seem satisfied and retrieve your pen. You unfold your original drawing and tell your friend to compare what she/he's drawn with your original. Your friend's drawing looks like this:

"Cripes," you exclaim. "Usually I can make people come closer than that. I guess there's a squiggle that looks a little like fingers, but . . . wait! Try holding it up to the mirror. Sometimes people think in mirror image."

Your friend holds the "drawing" up to the mirror. Here's what he/she sees:

"EXOD," you say. "What could that mean?"

If your friend has been raised in the western world, chances are she/he'll say, "Exodus? Could that be Exodus, chapter four, verse six?" Your friend will be delighted that her/his Sunday School training has paid off at last.

"Oh, I wish we had a bible to check it," you say innocently.

"But we do!" your friend says. "There's a Gideon bible right in the dresser drawer, dummy!"

Quickly your friend opens to Exodus 4:6 and reads:

' And he put his hand in his bosom, and when he took it out, behold, his hand *was* leprous, like snow.

Your friend compares your drawing and the passage from Exodus. A hand leprous as snow! "Amen," you say reverently.

AN ASIDE
BEFORE WE EXPLAIN
HOW IT'S DONE

Pause for a moment before you learn the secret, and reflect.

Your friend never saw your original drawing. From the time you handed your friend the pad and pen, you never again touched the paper. All you did was talk. Right? Right. It's a bloody miracle.

If a tabloid TV show (let's say, *Unexplained Untruths for the Uncritical*) broadcast the story of this trick, and if you were willing to lie a little, millions of people might learn about your mythical superpowers. If you were a real scumball, you'd let them believe, and soon the gullible and desperate would be spending their last $142.99 ordering your mind-power audiocassettes from late-night infomercials. You'd be rich and get your teeth capped.

Now, stop daydreaming. We know you're not a scumball. We've done the demographics and found that scumballs simply do not read Penn & Teller books. We know that if your friend asks, "Was it a miracle? Am I psychic?" you'll reply, "Of course not. There's no such thing. I'm just diabolically clever." You may not make a lot of friends or money with this presentation, but at least you're no weasel.

But the next time your local newspaper claims that a psychic in Sweden led the police to a killer, remember this trick. Ask yourself which is more likely: the laws of the known universe have been suspended; or some chiseler is doing a trick and lying about it to make money.

And don't give the weasels any great credit for being ingenious scamps. Scumballs don't get famous because they're more talented or clever than you. They're just willing to be scumballs, and — thank you very much — you're not.

AUTOMATIC WRITING?
WELL . . .

This trick looks like "automatic writing." That's what flimflam psychics do when they go into a "trance" and take memos from the vast beyond.

Not every automatic writer is a crook. Some are kooks who have convinced themselves that their pencils are directed by beings from another dimension. Sir Arthur Conan Doyle's wife once dropped into a trance and wrote Houdini a long, sappy message from his dead mother. When Houdini noticed that the message was in English (his mother spoke only German) and that Ma had directed Lady Doyle to draw a nice cross at the top of the note (Ma was Jewish, in fact the wife of a rabbi), Houdini was not impressed.

In our trick, however, your friend isn't really doing any writing at all. The "mirror image" squiggles are *already on the pad* when you hand it to your friend. And the pen you provide doesn't work. That's why your friend has to write on an unseen surface. Simple as that. And to think, just two column inches ago, this trick sounded like something Moses would have done to impress Pharaoh.

THE GIMMICKS

You'll need a ballpoint pen that doesn't write. If you're patient, you'll just wait to do this trick until your pen runs dry. If you want to perform this tomorrow night, there are shortcuts below. You'll also need a duplicate pen that works.

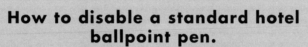

How to disable a standard hotel ballpoint pen.

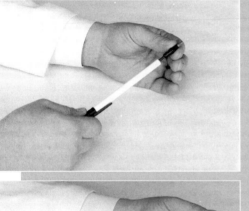

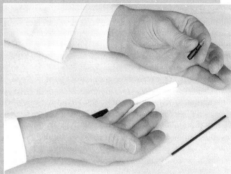

The pens most commonly supplied in hotel rooms come apart easily like this.

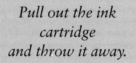

Pull out the ink cartridge and throw it away.

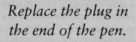

Replace the plug in the end of the pen.

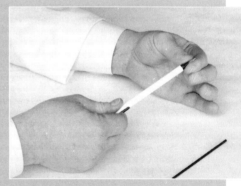

Then draw loop-de-loops on a piece of newspaper until the tip runs out of ink.

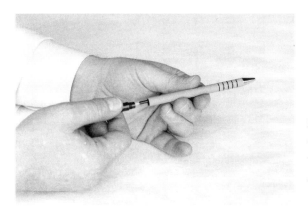

A Paper Mate Flexgrip is easy to turn into a gimmick, too. Just unscrew the plug at the end and pull out the ink cartridge. Yank out the tip with pliers and stick it into the *non-ink* end.

Now reassemble the pen and draw the aforementioned loopies until the tip runs dry.

**CAUTION:
Don't wear
a white linen suit
while doing
this preparation.**

The wobbly mirror writing is prepared ahead of time on the *second* page of the pad. Write in a wobbly hand, in mirror image. An easy way to do this is to put your pad under a tabletop (paper facing the floor) and hold your pen underneath. Then as you look down, trace the imaginary letters from beneath.

THE SETUP

Be sure your hotel has Gideon bibles in the rooms.

Plant the pad. If you're performing in your own hotel room, you're all set. If you're in your friend's room, prepare the pad from your night table and switch it for your friend's while he/she's not looking.

Have a working pen and the gimmicked dry pen on your person.

IMPORTANT NOTE: Don't be in a big hurry to take back the gimmicked pen. Act casual and wait for a moment when it seems natural. An ideal time is while your friend is all wrapped up in finding the Gideon bible and reading the passage.

THE STING

Introduce your trick by saying, "Want to see something really neat I learned to do from *Penn & Teller's How to Play in Traffic*, an opus of great personal and practical value to anyone who travels?" We suggest this opening line for three reasons: 1. If your friend is amazed, he'll buy our book and help us pay for our extravagant lifestyle. 2. Using our name gives you credibility. 3. If you say, "Wanna see a magic trick?" most people will shake their heads and turn on the TV.

If your friend agrees to watch, pick up the pad. Be sure your friend gets a good glimpse of the blank top page. Do *not* say, "This pad is blank." This is one of the most important principles of fooling an audience: Don't tell them what to believe. Show them something that lets them observe and come to their own wrong conclusion. If you say, "This pad is blank," they'll doubt you. They'll want to look the pad over. If you casually point to the pad and say, "I'm going to draw a picture, but I don't want you to know what it is," they will absorb the "fact" that the pad is blank and believe it without question.

"I'm going to draw a picture."

Now turn the pad so your friend can't see the page. Draw the picture of the creepy leprous hand with glow-lines coming off it. When you've finished, put away your pen (*very* important).

Then tear off the page with your picture and put it aside, facedown. Now, without exposing the second page, turn the pad facedown and put it in your friend's hand. If there's a table handy, you can even have him/her hold it under the table.

Now take out the dry pen (pretending it is the one you just used) and place it underneath, with its point against the paper.

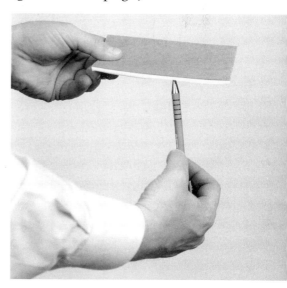

Ask your friend to relax and listen to your directions. What you say is easy to improvise, but we'll give you the general style: "Draw a short curve, now a straight line, now lift the pen and put it down a little distance away. Make three short strokes. Now an oval, now a small wavy line. Now let your hand take over for a few seconds and drift . . . " You are trying to make your friend completely lose track of what's being "drawn" so that later she/he will think he/she wrote what's on the pad.

When you think your friend has "drawn" enough, finish the trick as we've described under how it looks.

Don't forget to act disappointed when you first see the squiggles on the pad. Take your time "realizing" that there might be value to looking at the mirror image (if you give your friend a chance, maybe he/she will think of this). Again, act puzzled when you decipher the writing and let your friend get the idea to look it up in the Gideon bible. This makes everything seem more surprising and dramatic. Try to give your friend the impression that *you* are just making a drawing and talking a little, and that she/he is doing most of the work. People are always more amazed when they think the trick happened completely in their hands.

BOYO, DO WE DO OUR HOMEWORK

Now, sooner or later you'll want to find your favorite biblical passage to draw for this trick. The bible's full of spicy possibilities. The one we chose for the moguls (it was an adults-only party) is the shaven-headed sex-slave in bondage described in Deuteronomy 21:11–12. But the bible has quite a variety. So for starters, here are a few, ranging from the easy-to-draw and innocuous to the artistic and lurid.

In the event you're staying at a hotel that does not presume to force-feed religious literature, you can always do this trick with whatever other coffee-table pap they leave for your amusement. Have your "automatic writing" message guide you to a certain page and line of Conrad Hilton's autobiography or *Welcome to Philadelphia* magazine. If you know your friend always reads *USA Today*, pick up a copy at the gift shop and choose a tasty image of misery or mayhem.

FOR PEOPLE WITH NO ART SKILLS

YOU DRAW	BOOK, CHAPTER, VERSE OF BIBLE	TEXT
	Revelation 9:1	. . . and I saw a star fall from heaven unto the earth: and to him was given the key to the bottomless pit.
	James 1:10	. . . as the flower of the grass he shall pass away.
	Job 26:13	. . . his hand hath formed the crooked serpent.
	Deuteronomy 14:9	These ye shall eat of all that are in the waters; all that have fins and scales shall ye eat.
	Lamentations 3:12	He has bent his bow and set me as a mark for the arrow.
	Ezekiel 7:23	Make a chain: for the land is full of bloody crimes, and the city is full of violence.
	Ezekiel 10:13	As for the wheels, it was cried unto them in my hearing, O wheel!
	John 9:32	Since the world began was it not heard that any man opened the eyes of one that was born blind.
	John 19:17	. . . a place called the place of a skull, which is called in the Hebrew Golgotha.

MORE CHALLENGING

YOU DRAW	BOOK, CHAPTER, VERSE OF BIBLE	TEXT
	Deuteronomy 27:21	Cursed be he that lieth with any manner of beast . . .
	Luke 10:18	And he said unto them, I beheld Satan as lightning fall from heaven.
	Deuteronomy 19:5	As when a man goeth into the wood with his neighbour to hew wood, and his hand fetcheth a stroke with the axe to cut down the tree, and the head slippeth from the helve, and lighteth upon his neighbor, that he die; he shall flee unto one of those cities and live.

FOR ADULTS (OR YOUTHS WHO KNOW MORE THAN ADULTS THINK THEY DO).

If you want more ideas, try Song of Solomon, Chapter 7 or Ezekiel, Chapter 22 or any of the many other places where the prophets get explicit.

YOU DRAW	BOOK, CHAPTER, VERSE OF BIBLE	TEXT
Draw your own sexy picture.	Job 3:12	Why did the knees prevent me? or why the breasts that I should suck?
If you need help, check Dr. Spock.	Genesis 17:1	And ye shall circumcise the flesh of your foreskin . . .

AFTERMATH

The little club where we did the show for the moguls didn't have a Gideon bible, and we had told the organizers we needed one for our punch line. Now, when movie people need something in a hurry, they send out a production assistant — a young indentured servant trying to break into the movie business by running errands for bigwigs. So they sent a kid out to find a bible late on a Saturday night. He came back a few hours later with the only one he could find: his 200-year-old family bible. He handed it over to the organizers gingerly, saying, "They won't do anything bad to it, will they?" The organizers assured him we wouldn't.

Unfortunately, nobody told us. So when the guest of honor had read the biblical passage, we, in a burst of bravado, ripped out the page and handed it to him as a souvenir. It was years later before anybody mentioned it to us.

That kid's probably a mogul by now and waiting for his chance to do us dirt when we're pitching a script.

Or maybe he just has a great story to tell his kids about the psychos who wrecked the family bible. A missing page of Deuteronomy seems a small price. After all, what's more precious than scars you can brag about?

AH, FLORIDA — I REMEMBER THE PEPPERONI-LOVING "DANCER" WITH THE LATEX AREOLA AND THE UNDERWEAR ON HER HEAD
This isn't really a trick, it's more of a hint. Just think of us as the Heloises of the road.

MAIN STREET U.S.A. HAS BEEN EATEN BY the American Mall. You can travel a long way in this country and nothing changes. The bad things about American Mall-ville have been well documented. There's now an American homogeneity that takes a lot of the fun out of travel. From ME to HI, AK to TX, there's got to be a goddamn Banana Republic. You can get Kentucky Fried Chicken and Yankee Candles at the mall in Mississippi. It used to be *Boston* Baked Beans and *Mississippi* Mud Cake, now it's The *Country's* Best Yogurt. There are fewer and fewer site specific snacks and trinkets to show for your miles. They sell Empire State Building refrigerator magnets at Graceland.

The upside of Mall-ville is the same as the downside — homogeneity. If you have to travel a lot, any mall will feel familiar and comfortable. Business travelers and show-folk love malls. If you get disoriented and confused — just get yourself to the nearest mall and have some Cinnabon comfort food (you pig!).

As freedom and money spread, we can hope to live long enough to see American-style malls pop up all over our world, even in what's now called the Third World. Yeah, we'll lose a little culture and diversity, but it's a small price to pay for world health — there's no dysentery at Dillard's. No malaria at Macy's. Malls even bring peace. U.S. research has discovered that no two nations with McDonald's restaurants have ever gone to war. Belarus and Tahiti just brought the tally to 101 countries. That's millions *really* served. Thomas Friedman in the *New York Times* laid out The Golden Arches Theory of Conflict Prevention. It holds that countries can't support a McDonald's until they have reached a sufficient level of prosperity and political stability to make war unattractive to their people. Give peace a chance, with a side of fries.

So, if you want local memories as you travel, forget about shopping. Everyone already figures you picked up the spiffy cowboy hat at the Buffalo airport anyway. If you want to talk about local flavor, you're talking strip bars. If you want a memory that is county specific — strip clubs deliver. I'm calling them "strip clubs" after some thought. I will not call them "Gentlemen's Clubs" — that's just a lie. I will not name them after a specific sex or a sex-specific body part, because there are people of both sexes who go to see bodies of people of both sexes. All healthy people like to see other people naked. Some people have naked people running around their homes, and some people have to work harder to see sexy people. But we all like it. It's a fact of life. It doesn't take Richard Dawkins to figure out how a sexy obsession with naked bodies was selected by big, stupid, evolution. In the big picture, eating and breathing are nothing more than a way to hold out until sex. People say there's too much sex in entertainment. I'm always amazed that Penn & Teller can make a buck without sex in our show. We're crazy, we're kicking a dachshund uphill — sex is all that matters.

Entertainment in strip clubs can't be the same everywhere. You can make corn dogs and pretzels pretty near the same everywhere. Jeans is jeans. Maybe there are a lot of differences on a detail level among specific peaceful Micky D apple pies, but the untrained aren't going to notice. People are a whole different story. To people, people are unique right at first glance. People recognition and interest are hardwired. Yeah, sure, make some snide remark about silicon pecs, collagen lips, and hair extensions, but you know you're lying. Maybe *you* can't tell the *Baywatch* cast or the Village People apart without their hats, but most humans could.

In a free-market world, enterprising sexy people would find how to be the most lucratively attractive in the sex industry. A partial homogeneity of sexiness could develop. Entomologists can take a piece of cork and dress it up so it looks just enough like a bee to make another bee crazy thinking it's watching a real bee info-dance. You can stuff stuff under parts of your skin and humans will slip money in your underwear. There's a certain silhouette that will get most anyone going. Hardwired.

Once that sexy shape has the attention of your little monkey brain, you start to notice the other things. You look behind the eyes. You watch the way that sexy shape moves. You listen to what that sexy shape says. That's what you remember. Those are the things that are different in every person. The monkey brain turns the head, the human brain sees and hears. I was in New Orleans a few years ago — I grabbed a hamburger at a Burger King and ate it, that's all I remember of that hamburger — but there was this brunette in a Bourbon Street strip club with a well-placed tattoo that will dance in my mind forever. Her brown eyes and flame tattoos will always be New Orleans to me.

⊙ ⊙

Government should not meddle in our art and entertainment (A and E are the same things in my booklet). Govern less, govern better; you don't need me to tell you that. In the case of strip clubs, local government intrusion forces a way goofy sexual bio-diversity. We don't just have the differences from human to human, we have gross differences from county to county.

Local power-hungry creeps have done all sorts of surreal things to humans in the name of decency. The *California* vs. *LaRue* case claimed that the Twenty-first Amendment gave the government the ability to regulate nudity if liquor was involved. (If alcohol were to get near a primary or secondary sexual characteristic, all hell would break loose.) This gave us three strip clubs in St. Paul, Minnesota, each of which is two distinct street addresses separated by a glass wall. One address has a liquor license and the other is a "dance studio." The "dancers" dance nude at the "studio," while the drinkers watch them through the glass and slide tips through holes in the glass wall. It's sometimes billed as "The Best Ass under Glass," and it gives the uneasy feeling of going to a people zoo. It's kind of wonderful in its creepiness. I haven't found the county, but I've heard tell of a place in FLA where the law states that the "dancers" must wear underwear. It doesn't say where one has to wear them, so you'll see dancers shaking their bare money-makers with panties wrapped around their wrists.

⊙ ⊙

There are rules that eliminate live sex art entirely, like the rule that says "dancers" can't come within six feet of patrons and cannot be directly compensated (tipped). The reason? Ostensibly it stops prostitution and drug deals. I don't know anything about recreational drugs, I've never even had alcohol in my life, but it's hard for me to think of a harder way to make an illegal drug deal than naked with a crowd of people watching.

Local governments have paid lawyers to try to legally define "bra." They've ended up with a lot of "language of support," and some Jersey women tying red xmas ribbons under their mammoplasties. The Supreme Court said that pasties and a G-string (I'm glad that they have to humiliate themselves by using those silly words) don't infringe that much on the First Amendment (it makes my blood boil that it's okay to take our rights away a *little bit*).

The weirder the restrictions, the weirder the reaction. If the areola has to be covered, well, rubber freaks can see nipples encased in dried latex like a Jurassic insect in amber. There are fewer rules for male "dancers," because in many places, they just ban it outright. I guess the mostly male politicians figure no one would want to see *them* naked, so why should they see any male working it, girlfriend.

All this insane intrusion creates local community memories to go along with the individual memories. If that stripper, Gio, had been in Florida instead of Louisiana, I might have remembered the flame tattoo *and* plasticized nipples. I want to make it very clear: individual humans have enough genetic and artistic variation for city to city memories. I don't want to be misunderstood as saying anything good about these sick, nutty rules. I have great memories of East St. Louis, and I didn't notice any rules in effect there at all.

So it's about time to get to our travel hint. This idea comes from our dear friend, Michael Goudeau, star of the hit juggling show in Vegas that also features Lance Burton doing magic.

Michael points out that when going to a strip club, most of

us want attention from the dancers. It's not always that easy to get. A few single bills for tips is not going to do it; everyone has single bills. You could dress in a chicken suit, but that's the wrong kind of attention, and I'm sure there's a law on the books somewhere against people in poultry suits gawking at naked people.

When Michael walks into a strip club, he goes right to the pay phone and orders a large pizza to be delivered to him at the club. All the patrons have dollar bills; Goudeau has pizza. He gets attention.

So, as you travel this great land, go to strip clubs to get the local flavor and some site-specific memories. Walk in and invest some of your sex tip money in pizza. You'll get a lot of attention from the dancers and if you don't, who cares, you have pizza.

AYE JAYE'S MITT-CAMP WATCH DODGE

W E HAVE MADE SOME AMAZING FRIENDS as we've wandered these shores doing our little show. Hovering right up around the top of our list of favorites is our friend Aye Jaye.

Aye Jaye is a burly man in his fifties, with a booming voice and a disheveled smile. He is a former circus and carnival performer, but there really are no ex-carnies, only ones who move on to other, more up-to-date joints. So nowadays, Aye Jaye hits the circuit as stand-up comedian, motivational lecturer, and author of the book *The Golden Rules of Schmoozing*.

Aye Jaye

But back in his years traveling with circuses, Aye Jaye learned how to be a stranger in a strange town and have the populace end up either terrified of him or in love with him (to us, it's hard to tell those feelings apart).

He showed his talent for shrewd psychology even as a teenager, traveling with the sideshow. One night he was walking on a deserted street in an unknown town — not a safe thing for an outsider to do. Suddenly he found himself surrounded by local young toughs, ready to show him some bare-knuckled hospitality. Without blinking, Aye Jaye started talking *into his watch*. "No problem, cap'n," he said to his timepiece, "it's just kids." Then he turned to the gang and said with authoritative impatience, "Beat it, boys. This is a stakeout." They looked at one another for a moment, then ran away.

Nowadays as a lecturer, Aye Jaye often finds himself attending banquets. Sitting overdressed at a table with people you have nothing in common with is no treat. Aye Jaye has devised an ingenious way to turn that discomfort inside out. He begins by introducing himself, which prompts the others at the table to do the same. After a little chat, he suggests his scam: "Let's make this look like the best table at the whole banquet," he says to his new friends. "Let's pretend to be having such a good time that everybody else in the room will wish they were having a blast with us, instead of making polite conversation with Mormons." They ask what they should do. "Well, on the count of three," he says, "let's all act as though she," he points to one of the diners, "has just told the funniest story we've ever heard." He counts 1, 2, 3, and people burst out laughing and applauding and pointing to the diner Aye Jaye chose. She beams modestly and the glum banqueters at nearby tables look over at them jealously. Throughout the evening, Aye Jaye's party explodes with ersatz merriment and by the end of the banquet everyone in the room wishes they had sat with Aye Jaye. And the folks at his table, of course, have ended up having a wonderful time sharing the joy of conning the world.

Aye Jaye has a favorite magic trick. He never does it except when he's traveling. The trick begins hours before his audience realizes it. Aye Jaye says to the people he's visiting, "Folks, would you take me out someplace tonight, but don't tell me where we're going? I want you to surprise me. Take me to a restaurant I've never been to before."

When they arrive and are sitting around the table, Aye Jaye offers to show them "a talent I learned back when I was with the mitt camp." A mitt camp is the professional term for a palm reader's premises, a place where your livelihood is sizing up your customers.

Aye Jaye begins by borrowing a watch that can be set easily by turning its stem. He says, "Now, I've never been here before, and you all know that's true. Pick out one of the waiters or waitresses, any one at all, and bring him or her over to the table." The server comes over and Aye Jaye introduces himself. He asks the server's name and a few incidental questions like, "How long have you worked here? Are you married? What month were you born?" All the time he's talking, he's looking the server over carefully, inspecting the fingernails, the shoes, the haircut. He sometimes asks to examine the inside of the server's left palm and wrist, where the skin wrinkles, and with true mitt-camp flair mutters, "Ooh. Can't tell you about that now. Wait until next fall."

Then he says, "I want you to take this watch into the kitchen and set it to any time of the day you want to. Then wrap it back up in the napkin so nobody sees it but you." Then he takes a napkin and folds the watch up inside it and hands it to the waitperson, who goes to the kitchen.

Aye Jaye thinks for a moment, then takes a matchbook or piece of paper and writes something on it. With a flourish, he slaps it, writing-side down, onto the table and puts a salt shaker on top of it. He then reminds his companions that they chose the restaurant and the server, so there is no way Aye Jaye could plan anything in advance.

The server returns, hands the watch wrapped in the napkin to one of Aye Jaye's fellow diners, and gets on with his/her work. Aye Jaye asks the person with the watch to open the napkin and announce the time it's set to. When they turn over the paper under the salt shaker, the time — set by a total stranger — matches exactly.

The trick is perfect: simple, practical, nearly foolproof, and based on the showbiz axiom that humans universally enjoy making monkeys of their fellow men.

Before he goes on any trip, Aye Jaye makes up several little packets that look like this: ▶

NOTE: *This is the exact wording Aye Jaye uses. Now, if we had written it, we would have put something in about "keep the secret," but neither of us has ever worked in a mitt camp, so we advise you to do it just as Aye Jaye says.*

When Aye Jaye sits down at the table in the restaurant, he sneaks his little note-packet into his lap. When the time comes to fold the watch into the napkin, he drops his right hand into his lap, picks up the packet, and holds it casually hidden in the hand. He takes up three corners of the napkin in his other hand, then picks up the watch and tucks it inside (secretly adding his note-packet). Immediately he picks up the fourth corner and gathers it with the other two, forming the kind of bundle storks deliver babies in, and hands it to the server.

That's all there is to the mechanics. What sells it is the acting.

When he seems to be studying the server's appearance and asking his questions, it's all part of the act, designed to suggest that he can deduce a person's decisions from a manicure.

He says the only time this trick fails is if the server doesn't speak reasonably fluent English. Once in a Thai restaurant the waitress returned giggling and puzzled, waving the note and the money stapled to it. It bombed as a trick, but succeeded as comedy.

However, as long as the message is understood, Aye Jaye assures us the secret is safe — guarded by the carny instinct latent in everyone's heart.

STRANGERS ON A TRAIN

D O Y O U R E C A L L T H E G A M E (popular during puberty) in which two people stare at each other and the first one to laugh loses? If you were a winner in that game, this item should be right up your alley.

We picture it in use on a train (mostly because we like stealing the title of an old Hitchcock movie) but it's good on planes or buses, too — any time you're stuck next to a stranger for a little too long.

"Excuse me," you say. "I just wanted to mention that during long rides I sometimes fall asleep with my eyes open. It's nothing harmful. I've done it since I was a kid. It's just a regular nap and I feel fine afterwards. But if I happen to nod off, please don't be worried. I'm not dead."

Phase I

Now you let some time pass, say an hour. Then, gradually, you let your jaw go slack and slump back in your seat with your eyes open.

Sooner or later your seatmate will notice. She or he will try not to stare, but it's hard. This is a severe test of your staring-down skill. Remember the mantra of the old-time comedians: "It'll be funny tomorrow."

If you pass that hurdle, then you can move on to Phase II. Shift in your "sleep,"

Phase II

so that your head rolls towards your seatmate and your eyes are staring straight into his/hers like a dead fish.

Hold this pose until your seatmate has moved or found a way to avoid your moribund stare. Then shift to another position, and, a few moments later, "wake up."

Stretch. Yawn. Sigh. Act refreshed.

Do *not* comment. Take out a book and read. Pretend it never happened.

This is a favorite travel pastime of magician Mac King.

Mac King

INIDUOH: SEXY LITTLE BACKWARDS HOUDINI SHOWER TRICK

HERE'S ANOTHER "MELISSA ETHERIDGE, Uma Thurman, Mel Gibson, & Jaye Davidson Trick" for really attractive people. The rest of us may also find it useful. Even if you're as ugly as the bottom of a foot, there's bound to be a time you can make use of a shower trick. All you need is to be around when someone's going to take a shower. You don't have to be in the shower with her or him. As a matter of fact, you *can't* be in the shower with him or her. For the trick to work, you have to be locked outside the bathroom while the victim showers. That's not an unusual situation for some of us.

It's great — you don't need to practice, you just need to do it. Here's how it looks: You're in a hotel room (it could be a private home, but, hey, it's a travel book) with your babe. (To keep with the tone of the Melissa-Uma-Mel-Jaye feel of this section of the book, I'm going to pretend you're doing this trick for your special friend du jour, but as you read, you'll see how it'll work just as well for your Trekkie roommate at the sci-fi convention.) It's shower time. Whether it's a before or after sex shower is up to you and your love partner. It's hard to forget that great quote from Napoleon to Josephine, "Home in three days. Don't wash." The quote may be apocryphal, but the spirit is dead on.

As your love is heading to the shower, you tell her or him that you have all the same skills as Houdini, but backwards. You can break *in* to any place. Explain that you don't use the skill much, because locks are for honest people (it's true [at least this one tiny part]: bad people just break down the door) and you respect that. Ask if he or she will allow you to demonstrate your skill. Ask her or him for permission to violate her or his privacy (see, it *is* a pretty sexy trick). Look at the bathroom lock and point out how it works. Say it's a really easy one. Don't brag on the B&E part of this too much; almost anyone can break into an hotel bathroom — it's just a privacy set. But you'll do better. You will break in, watch your play-mate shower, and sneak back out without being seen. It's impressive: there aren't that many places to hide in a bathroom.

Tell him or her to go in, lock the door, take a nice hot shower, and the whole time keep his or her eyes peeled. You promise you'll be in and out without being seen.

Let's assume your sex machine will do as she or he is told (at least as far as this request is concerned; as far as the rest of your relationship, that's your business). Your stud or filly will lock the door and shower while staring at the door. It'll give her or him a weird *Psycho* vibe. When he or she comes out of the shower — there's the proof. This message is written in the fog on the bathroom mirror: ▶

That message is just a suggestion, you don't have to write that. Write whatever you want. Pick any body part you like and make the appropriate comment. For those of us who aren't really in the Melissa-Uma-Mel-Jaye category, we might want to write: ▶

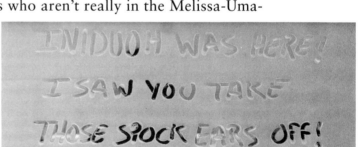

She or he sees the message, checks the door, and it's locked. It's an okay trick. For the amount of work you have to put in, it's a *great* trick. You just need to be in the bathroom alone, before your honey showers. When you're in there, unwrap the little bar of hotel soap and write the message on the mirror with soap.

To write on the mirror, just dip your finger in water, rub it on the soap and write with your finger. Keep a high percentage of water in the mix. You don't need much soap, your solution should be fairly dilute. You can try using the bar itself to write, but you have to write *really* lightly. Writing with the bar often puts too much soap on the mirror and you'll have to wipe it off lightly with the towel.

We'll say we both snuck in! ▶

Just wipe it off enough so the writing won't show until the shower fogs the mirror. (That's why you tell your sweetie to take a hot shower. If you're with someone who takes cold showers, find a new lover. That's just too stupid.) It doesn't have to be completely invisible; your sex king or queen won't be trying to read the mirror. Take your time; you can write it as much in advance as you want as long as you do the trick before the next maid service. Maids usually wash the mirror.

    That's all that's to it. It's an easy, sexy little trick.

(A note to the less sexy — yeah, yeah, we know — it would be such a better trick if you really got to sneak into any shower you wanted without being seen. But look on the bright side, maybe you can convince the geek that you already saw everything and she or he will let you watch her or him get dressed in their *Enterprise* uniform.)

Hey, wait! Guess what? This could also be a card trick.

If you're sexy enough to pull off the Iniduoh thing, you'll have no trouble pulling off a card trick. And, if you're doing it for a geek — geeks love card tricks. We don't have to walk you through this do we? You can figure it. Wait until your fox is on the way to the shower and whip out a deck of cards. Do the envelope card force on pages 5–7 with your favorite card. Make sure they look at the card before they seal it up. Take the sealed envelope, with their "freely selected" card inside and hold it to your forehead. Concentrate hard and say, "You have sealed a random card in this envelope. I will now tell you the name of that card." Make those universal concentration faces and say, "You have chosen the Queen of Diamonds" (name any card that *isn't* the card you made them pick.) When they tell you that it wasn't the card you named, say, "I screwed up, I'm sorry. Go ahead, take your hot shower. Take your card in your sealed envelope in the bathroom with you, I don't even want to look at it. Maybe you can wash off the stink of my stinky trick."

When he or she comes out of the shower, the punch line will be waiting. He or she will think you snuck in, opened the envelope, peaked at the card, resealed the envelope, and wrote on the mirror. It's impressive and it's pretty sexy. For a card trick it's *way* sexy.

THE FIVE CENT KOAN

AN AIRPORT CAN BE A SANCTUARY for philosophers. There may be tinny loudpeakers and beeping carts, and masses of humanity screaming, kissing, arguing, and gobbling. But if you know where to look, an airport is as good a place as the Himalayas for contemplating the big picture.

The following is not like the tricks you use to baffle other people. You use it to fool yourself. We call it the Five Cent Koan, because its paradoxical nature reminds us of those riffs (e.g., "What is the sound of one hand clapping?") Zen followers believe short-circuit the path to enlightenment. We make no such claims — to us enlightenment is reading a good book. But if you try the Five Cent Koan, you may find yourself unexpectedly grinning like a Tibetan monk while your fellow travelers fret their trips away.

Take out a nickel (or a penny, if you have a tight budget for epiphany) and memorize it. Study the date, the markings, the tarnish. Let your hand get the feel of the weight, the temperature, the knurl of the edge.

Now find a moving sidewalk, a nice long one. Most concourses in large airports have them. Wait until there's a little break in the pedestrian traffic. Then place your nickel on the black handrail that moves with the sidewalk. Stay where you are, and watch your coin glide away.

As it retreats, think to yourself: My nickel is vanishing into oblivion.

Gradually and visibly, the coin will seem to fade, melt, and dissolve into the handrail. Before long the nickel will completely disappear.

Now, you know from experience that things don't really vanish. You realize that as the distance between you and the nickel increases, the coin becomes less and less visible, masked by the reflections on the shiny black top of the handrail. And yet the illusion is so perfect . . .

Wait at least sixty seconds (perhaps use the time to wash your hands in the rest room; the more often you wash your hands the less likely you are to pick up a cold at the airport — a travel tip that has nothing to do with this trick). Then get on the moving sidewalk yourself. Ride it to the end. When you get off, look around. Search the floor.

The nickel will be gone.

Now, as you sit in the waiting area, reflect. Common sense tells you that when the coin came to the end of the railing, it must have fallen off and been picked up and pocketed by a stranger.

But your eyes insist that you saw the coin vanish into oblivion.

Which will you believe: what you thought you saw or what you think you know?

Sir Arthur Conan Doyle, novelist and ardent believer in fairies and spirit realms, would declare in no uncertain terms that the coin had surely slipped into another

dimension. Sir Arthur was confident that if he could not instantly see how an illusion worked, it could not be an illusion.

Aristotle, arguing from the general to the specific, would reason that since people act in their own self-interest, somebody no doubt snatched up the coin and used it towards the purchase of a pack of gum.

Madame Curie, we imagine, would have invested another nickel, and this time trotted alongside the moving sidewalk to see for herself whether there were any new chemical principles in operation.

So now it's time to make your choice. Will you answer the mystery with faith, reason, or sleuthing?

Someday your nickel will come back. You'll see.

But meanwhile, as you sit waiting, reconstruct the lost coin in your mind. Picture the tarnish and markings. Let your hand recall the temperature, the knurls of the edge against your skin. Take your time, and when the imaginary reconstruction of the nickel is complete, ask yourself: has the nickel really disappeared from your life or — because you can re-create it so vividly — is it still yours?

If it's still yours, take it to the newsstand. See what it will buy.

Remember when you were in sixth grade and the kid in the schoolyard punched you in the shoulder until you were ready to kill him? At the time it seemed like the end of your life. But now, where has he gone?

He rode the black handrail into oblivion. Just like the coin, he went farther and farther away until he was no longer part of your world.

Perhaps he's dead. Or perhaps he moved on to a different life: now he's a drill sergeant in South Carolina or a photog-

rapher in Bosnia or a hairdresser in Dallas. It's all the same to you.

Unless, that is . . . unless he's right there at the very airport where you made your nickel disappear. Maybe he got on the moving sidewalk just after you put your nickel on the handrail, and picked up the coin when it fell. Maybe he's sitting next to you right now. He'd be hard to recognize from the old days. Look around. Is that him?

And what's that glinting in the bastard's hand? Your god-damn nickel?

The next time you get off a moving walkway at an airport, look down. You may find a gift from another reader of this book: a coin, sent by handrail, care of oblivion.

We told you it would come back someday. Spend it wisely.

Teller claims that when he tries the Five Cent Koan the nickel vanishes. Penn says he always finds the nickel waiting at the far end of the walkway. Such contradictions have fueled Penn & Teller's partnership for over twenty years.

If you try this trick and, like Penn, find your coin lying by the end of the walkway, don't be disappointed. Celebrate. You've just made five cents.

Made five cents? Sure. When you put your nickel on the handrail, you resigned yourself to the fact that it was gone, spent on a frivolous philosophical experiment. You might just as easily have spent that nickel on candy or used it towards the purchase of a limousine. You could have lost it in the stock market or paid for part of your movie ticket with it. It's the way of life, spending, losing. So that nickel was gone.

Then you got off the moving sidewalk, and suddenly you were five cents richer than you were just moments earlier. The nickel was an unexpected windfall. Congratulate yourself on your talent for being in the right place at the right time. Be proud. Pick up the coin and exclaim, "Hey, who says you never get something for nothing! Look what I found! Luck is my lady tonight!"

So you have a no-lose situation: If the coin is gone, you win a mystery. If the coin is there, you win the envy of your fellow travelers.

We like our metaphysics with a money-back guarantee.

IT'S A HAT, SO IT'S FUNNY, RIGHT?

W E HAD A LOT OF IDEAS FOR THIS BOOK. The people we work with had a lot of ideas for this book. Our friends had a lot of ideas for this book. Look at the list of "thank-yous" (don't really look at the list of "thank- yous," no one really reads that page unless one is looking for one's own name): a lot of people had ideas.

We wanted still more. We went to SinCity. SinCity is the Penn & Teller web site. It's great and we have nothing to do with it. Our good friend, Maggie (she'll find *her* name in the "thank-yous"), posted lots of messages asking for P&T-type travel tricks.

Well, our friends on the Net came through. There was a suggestion for a *How to Play in Traffic* version of "Russian Roulette" that involved crossing the street without looking (maybe even a worse idea than the airplane security trick) and an idea for pasting hardcore pornography into Gideon's bibles (delightful idea, but we already had two bible tricks).

A guy named Charles Hardin sent us a quick e-note about a way wacky trick that he did while traveling through La Grange, Texas. He was in Weiner's clothing store when he saw a stranger coincidentally wearing a kind of hat that was on sale in that very store. Some crazy-monkey-muse filled Charles and, without thinking or planning, he grabbed a similar hat from a rack and ran up behind the behatted stranger. As he jogged by the hatman, he tapped him lightly on the hat, and continued to run, wildly waving the duplicate hat in the air and screaming like a nut. (We may not have needed to use a simile there. It's possible Charles Hardin may *be* a nut.)

Our innocent hat-wearing shopper assumed, of course, that he was the victim of a jog-by-hat-swipe and gave Mr. Hardin chase. After they ran for a little way we had the moment of comedy: at

some point, during his pursuit of our ersatz thief, Mr. Hat reached
up and hesitantly put a hand to the top of his head. He had a befud-
dling sensation: he felt his very own hat still perched on his very own
head. It's a way funny moment. Way funny.

Charles didn't know what was going to happen next, but to be
safe, he kept running. Good thinking. After Hatman's brief psychedelic hatcheck pause, he resumed the chase. No longer chasing a

thief who merely ripped off his hat, he was now chasing a thief who
stole his shopping serenity and dignity. Charles kept hauling
towards the exit. Right before hitting the exit, he dropped the hat
onto another rack (after all, he's not a shoplifter, he's a nut) and flew
out the store.

Charles didn't stop to look back again until he was in his car
driving away, leaving the man, hat on head, shaking his fist and
threatening like the surreal Three-Stooged fall guy he was.

We think this is really funny. We don't think the situation will come up very often. But there may be more opportunities for this gag than we think. It doesn't *have* to be a haberdashery, it doesn't even have to be a retail outlet — maybe you'll get lucky and your very own, privately owned hat will match the dupe's. Keep this gag in the back of your head, and if you ever find yourself around a guy with a hat while you have access to a duplicate . . . We don't know, it might be a good laugh.

What the hell — do it for Charley.

Please make sure your car starts right up. You're not *really* doing anything wrong, I guess, but — well, there's something very not right about it. If you're caught, you could be severely punished. And if Mr. Hatguy does catch you and beat you senseless . . . well, I'm not sure he could be convicted by a jury of his hat-wearing peers.

THE PRICE OF ADMISSION

WHEN I WAS A KID, I HAD A MAGIC CATALOG full of machinery that promised to make me worthy of an audience. The mysterious gadgets were said to confer — by their mere purchase — abilities which would otherwise require years of painful practice. The illustrations in the catalog were awe-inspiring. The suave performers radiated lines of amazement. Glowing question marks swirled upwards from their props. Thunderbolts shot from their commanding eyes and smoke exploded from their fingertips. One could almost hear the applause.

I saved my allowance, and I bought my show. The first thing I got was the Dream of Wealth, a device "precision machined" from paper clips and safety pins to allow one to harvest aluminum coins from the air, "No Skill Required!" Next in my hoard was a Temple Screen, an "apparently ordinary miniature Chinese folding screen" which, though shown "unmistakably empty on both sides," would produce colorful streamers and compressible cloth fruit — conveniently offered for sale in the "Production Items" section of the catalog. A birthday check from my grandparents brought me "Multum in Parvo" (the quaint Latin title means "Much in Little"), which enabled me to squeeze a pitcher ("much") of milk into a shot glass ("little"). One particularly profitable yuletide, I pooled the cash from all my relatives and invested in a "Zombie," a shiny metal ball that floats in the air

with "no threads or wires," provided nobody is watching from behind.

I loved buying tricks. Even today, I can't think of a greater thrill than exchanging my savings for a chrome-plated secret that bestowed on me the power to fascinate.

But, alas, by the time I entered high school, I had lost faith in the ability of props — however expensive — to make the amazement lines (so beautifully drawn in the catalog) radiate from me. My peers had ceased to be awed by my Temple Screen. It looked to them like what it was: cardboard and tape with Day-Glo Buddhas stapled on. An audience of Cub Scouts had thrown things at me and smashed my Multum in Parvo — "much in little," indeed!

So I shifted to a different vein of magic. I joined the Dramatics Club. Mr. Rosenbaum, our drama coach, was a serious man of the theatre. He

taught us stage techniques: how to sit on a chair or put on a coat gracefully so as not to distract from the dialogue; how to breathe from the diaphragm so the voice would carry; how to ask questions of a script and understand the motives of a character.

To the surprise of the school administration (who, I imagine, had expected the club to mount *Bye Bye, Birdie!*) Mr. Rosenbaum announced we'd be doing a performance of Sophocles' masterpiece *Oedipus Rex*. The preparation was epic. We studied the play until we understood every word — even the wacky choral odes. And Mr. Rosenbaum didn't let us act for free. We had to earn it. We had to audition.

I spent days preparing. I wanted the magician role in it, Teiresias, the blind soothsayer who in a rage tells Oedipus that, unknown to him, he's killed his dad and slept with his own mom. Strong stuff. I memorized the lines; I wanted to deliver them with my eyes closed — blind. The tryouts were held in a classroom, our chairs pulled in a circle around Mr. Rosenbaum's desk. Gaunt, mustachioed, he removed his glasses, rested his index finger on the bridge of his nose, and listened to our readings with the concentration of a doctor sounding a patient's lungs.

My main competitor for the role of Teiresias was formidable, an older kid with a deep voice and a lot of experience playing aged characters. He read with great power and authority. Then it was my turn. When I finished, Mr. Rosenbaum said, "Now do it again, but this time, don't worry about age or voice or pacing. Teiresias is first and foremost a seer. See. See what he is seeing, and then, and only then, let the words describe what you see." He was, in a single stroke, giving me an acting lesson and testing my ability to take direction.

The following afternoon, I went to the bulletin board to read the cast list, and opposite TEIRESIAS I found my name. Years later, when I had gone professional and Rosey and I had become good friends, I asked him why he picked me. He took a puff on his long, black, gold-tipped Soubranie cigarette and said simply, "You saw."

My school's budget for extracurricular drama was no dream of wealth. For a stage-setting we could barely afford a Temple Screen, much less a Greek temple. Rosey turned that to advantage. The chorus sat in jury-like chairs filched from the faculty lounge and King Oedipus addressed his subjects (played, to their surprise, by the audience) from the principal's podium. What little money we had went into renting tuxedos — plain formal wear in place of ancient robes — quite a shock to me, who had pictured Teiresias dressed like a ragged prophet. But the tuxedos worked magic. They stripped away everything but the passion in our little Stanislavskian hearts. It was *multum in parvo*.

In the last week of rehearsal, we stayed late, dined on burgers and milk shakes, and staggered home like zombies — not the chrome kind. When the performance came, and the audience not only clapped but cried at the saddest parts, I felt like I was inside one of the magic catalog's drawings, a halo of wonder surrounding the stage.

When you go to theatre, you pay for your ticket, but those who perform pay, too. Whether trading their treasure for store-bought secrets or bloodying their minds on the cliffs of Sophocles, they pay — and joyfully. The cellist pays with proud blisters on the fretful fingertips. The fashion model pays with heroic hours on the Soloflex. I'm paying right now — I've written seven drafts. But if I get it right, I know there is a chance this page might glow.

I've told you all this so you won't be surprised to find that in the following trick, you pay. A little or a lot, that's up to you. How much is it worth to incandesce? Turn the page and decide for yourself.

$ Picture this: You are in an airport, a bus station, an amusement park. "Got a dollar bill?" you say to your friend. If she/he does, you wink and invite your friend into the rest room. Uneasy suspense commences.

Together you step into a toilet stall. The uneasiness mounts.

You snatch your friend's bill, rip it to pieces, and hand one piece to your friend as a "receipt." Then, with no false moves, you flush the rest down the toilet. Your friend actually sees the pieces of the bill disappear down the drain. One kind of uneasiness replaces another.

You scurry out of the rest room before security officers start asking questions.

Outside, you summon the bill back from the depths and tell your friend to check his or her pockets. But alas, no bill. Instead your friend finds a locker key with a number on it. You appear baffled.

Together you locate the public lockers. When your friend opens the one that matches the key, voila! there is the bill, soaking wet and perfectly restored — except for one missing piece. Your friend remembers the "receipt." It fits perfectly.

$ This trick will cost you at least a buck and change. Begin by taking a bill from your own wallet and tearing out a little piece like this:

Even if you are not doing a trick, tearing money is fun.

$ Put the small piece in your pocket and wet the rest of the bill thoroughly at a wash basin or drinking fountain. Then find an empty locker and put the waterlogged bill inside. Close the locker and make your second investment, the key rental. (Note how carefully I avoid "dating" this book. I wisely leave out the locker-rental fee, so that when inflation hits, I won't get stuck rewriting. I wish I'd done that with the Soloflex allusion above. In ten years — this book is intended for the ages — no one will remember that Soloflex was a home exercise gizmo relentlessly advertised on late-night TV.)

Take the locker key and go in search of your audience.

Now, ordinarily you'd have your pick of possible spectators, but in this trick you must be a good judge of character. You have to find a friend willing and able to go to the toilet with you. As a rule, look for someone of your own sex, or at least someone who can pass for your own sex, or whose sex you can pass for. (I would pause here to question the wisdom of legislating the sexual segregation of public rest rooms — after all the same equipment suffices for both sexes in the home — but I think that would try your patience after the overlong Soloflex parenthesis above.)

Having found your audience, you must sneak the locker key into her or his pocket/purse/bosom without being caught. It's not hard, since few people take precautions against having valuables given to them. A man wearing a sport coat is a sitting duck. Sidle up to him and slide the key into the outer jacket pocket. To load a man's or woman's trouser pocket, arrange to stand in a snack bar line behind your target, and sneak in the key when they reach for the pie. It's helpful to choose a moment when your friend is distracted (or, of course, you can provide your own distraction by bumping into your friend nice and hard, and loading the pocket as you apologize). Remember, all that matters is that the key ends up on the his/her person. Be ruthless. Get inspired.

$ If for some reason you fail (e.g., your pal is zippered into Spandex), don't despair. Just place the key in your own wallet and begin the trick by ostentatiously handing your wallet to your friend and saying mysteriously, "Guard this with your life." If you suspect he/she might abscond, slip the key into something you can afford to lose (say, a greeting card you buy at a souvenir shop).

Now have your amigo get out a bill and follow you to the toilet. *Pointer*: Don't wait until you're in the loo to ask for the money or you might get stuck with the wrong denomination or a handful of quarters, which totally screws your preparation.

As you walk in, casually retrieve the torn-out piece of bill from your pocket. Invite the bill-bearer into the stall. Snatch his or her bill and, holding the extra piece *under* it, tear it in half, then tear the resulting halves in half twice more.

Meanwhile, sing out merrily, "Okay, now say along with me, 'Easy come! Easy go!'"

If you are poetically inclined, we suggest you substitute the following lyric, adapted from Thomas Dekker (1572–1632).

> "Money is trash, and he that will spend it,
> Let him live merrily; fortune will send it."

$ The money-lender chants with you. Now you peel off the extra piece you sneaked in and hand it to her/him as if it were one of the pieces you just tore. Say, as if it just happens to strike you funny, "Here's your receipt!" It's important that this "receipt" business look totally spur-of-the moment, as if you've just thought of a way to add insult to injury.

Drop the torn pieces into the toilet and flush. Inwardly rejoice in the knowledge that you are solvent enough to flush money down the toilet and still be free from want.

Look up at the appalled lender and say, "Now give me a hundred." Laugh heartily and exit the rest room. The work is done. All that's left is to relish the devastating denouement.

Play out the next moments as sadistically as you can without appearing smug. Pretend the trick is over. Talk about your health, the weather, the latest Washington scandal. When inevitably your friend raises the question of the return of the money, act surprised. Insist on doing another trick.

Make clawing motions at the floor, as if drawing the bill from the bowels of the earth, and recite, "Easy go! Easy come!" (or the second line of the Dekker poem, "Let him live merrily; fortune will send it"). Then say, "Now turn in a circle three times, then check your pockets."

Your pal does. When the key is discovered, act surprised, as if you expected the missing bill to be there. You won't fool anyone, but it's more polite than snickering.

Let your chum figure out that the key belongs to a locker and let him/her lead you there. When she/he opens the door and finds the wet bill, act surprised. Watch as the idea dawns on your *compadre* to check and see if the "receipt" fits the gap. Naturally, it does. You've bought yourself a condo on Olympus.

Electronic locker directions: Plant your bill in the locker, put in your rental money, and the machine will print a little slip showing the location, number, and secret entry code. Then take your choice:

1. Follow the directions above, sneaking the slip into the pocket just as you would a conventional key.

2. Replace the bills in your wallet with the little slip. After you've destroyed the money, take out your billfold as if you are about to reimburse the victim, then look startled and take out the slip and let your friend figure out the rest.

3. Get flamboyant. Instead of giving your friend the paper slip, memorize it, then go into a trance and "sleepwalk" to the bank of lockers. There, collapse in a heap on the floor, and scream out the combination in an *Exorcist*-style demon voice. When your friend enters the digits and the door electronically pops open, there will be no doubt the devil was at work.

```
       Las Vegas
       McCarran
        Airport

CABINET      LOCKER
  001          06

FOR THE RECOVERY
OF YOUR BAGGAGE.
TYPE THE CODE:

    689942

1997/03/11        9:27 PM
```

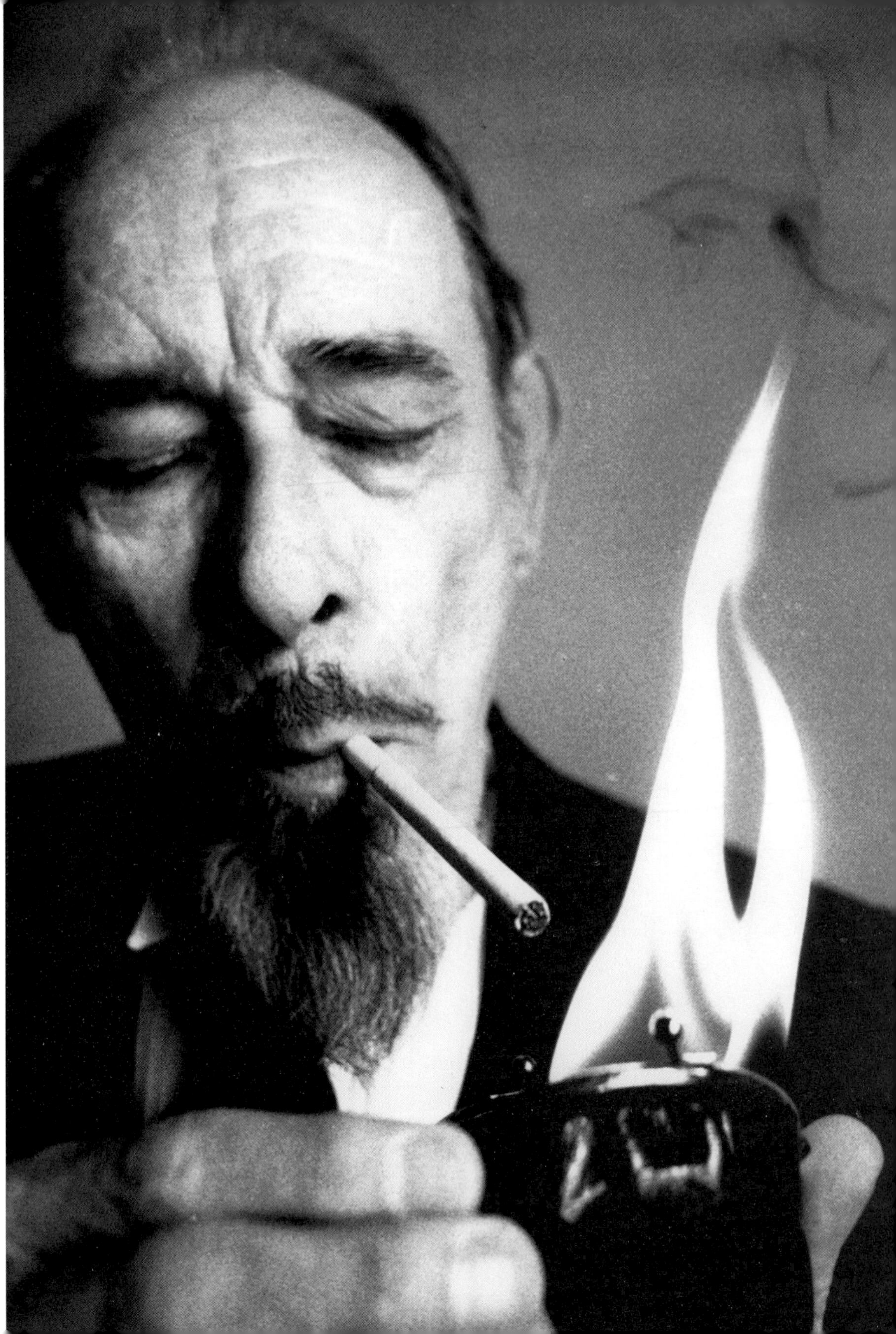

Mr. Rosenbaum used to quote Ezra Pound's axiom: The Obscene is the Root of the Sublime. Violence and sex-gone-bad are the heartbeat of the greatest classical tragedies. In this trick, we celebrate the most obscene act of our daily lives, the flush of a toilet. When the bill reappears wet, the implications are obvious. So play it lightly and gracefully. Avoid crass bathroom-humor commentary on what everyone already knows. If you think of the bill's destruction and resurrection as a genteel jest, the power of the subtext of the trick will hook in deep and make the effect — as Ezra might put it — sublime.

We know some readers will never try this trick. Though they unhesitatingly pay their buck-and-change to play a video game or eat an ice cream bar, they balk at the act of deliberately throwing away money for fun. They lack perspective.

You, however, see the possibilities. In fact, unless we miss our guess, you are right now considering using a five or ten or even a twenty-dollar bill (depending on your budget). You realize that as the value of the bill increases, so does the power of the trick. Not only does your sap have more at stake, but nobody, we repeat, nobody will believe you're nuts enough to flush away twenty bucks just to wow your audience.

But you aren't nuts at all. You just know the truth: To blaze in glory, you have to feed the flame.

Mr. Rosenbaum. Make him proud.

THE DEVIL WENT TO BELL LABS

THE DEVIL OFTEN APPEARS TO MORTALS in various narrative-convenient supernatural forms — genies, elves, gnomes, powerful drunks, etc. — and offers the protagonist a number of wishes. That number is usually three — when you're talking short stories, comedy, and Beelzebub, things work in threes (Joseph Campbell would have pretended that meant something). The poor protagonist sap makes a couple/three wishes and, with a poof, gets them granted. The wily antagonist keeps his promise within the grade-school rules of fairness and the hero ends up in worse shape than before. The maliciously literal granting of wishes has filled ages of entertainment with old, decrepit people that can't die, useless, tortuous told-ya-so rights, and a zillion twelve-inch pianists. In one fell swoop, the reader gets to covet the wishes and then be glad he didn't get them. An amusing way of reinforcing the status quo.

The devil, having spent human history appearing to a multitude of inarticulate, impulsive, down-and-out, hubris-filled chumps (the same brain-dead hicks that extraterrestrials are so fond of buzzing), decided to hit Bell Labs in Murray Hill, New Jersey, and rattle a few geek chains. A new kind of fun.

On the day, one of the "people-persons" employed by Bell Labs to call himself an executive was giving a "V.I.P. Tour" of the research facilities. Real Very Important People are never called V.I.P.'s, they are called, well, by their names. It was just after noon in the old Unix room and Mr. Exec was pointing out one of *the* guys responsible for the Internet to the group of executive suits from a distant land. This Internet genius was a guy sitting at a computer, drinking coffee and moving his mouse with small accurate movements. Our visionary looked up at the multitude of V.I.P.'s, smiled a surprisingly non-condescending smile, and silently raised his coffee cup in salutation. This is the big computer stop on the Bell Labs V.I.P. tour. If they wanted excitement, they should have gotten a tour of NASA; at least there you see a picture of really little, maybe Martian dead life, really big things that were damaged in space, *and* guys drinking coffee.

With the *turistas* gone, the only sounds in the Unix room were someone steaming whole milk on the professional cafe-quality espresso machine and the soft treble of a personal stereo blaring Pat Metheny into wireless headphones. There was no longer the noise of hard disks whirring or even typing. The big disk jukebox wasn't in this room, and mouses were quiet as mice. The phone rang. The phone doesn't really ring, the phone announces a name and, after years of getting used to it, only the named person bothers to hear it.

"William," intoned the telephone's digital voice, and Bill's computer screen opened a caller I.D. window that read, "908-555-7758 — Steven Jenkins."

Bill picked up the phone. "Hey, Stevie. You're back."

"Yeah, I just got back. My flight was fifty-one minutes *early*. We got a tail wind."

"Get some sleep. Go to sleep, man. That's a long flight."

"No alcohol, lots of water, and I walked during plane changes. I won't have much jet lag. It seems to be better if I don't sleep. I might just come into the lab today and try to get right back on Eastern Standard Time. I don't want to spend three days adjusting."

"What's the time difference?"

"Eight and a half hours. It's 8:38 p.m. to my circadian right now."

"Eight and a half?"

"Yeah, countries don't have to be on an even hour. I think it's either Suriname or French Guiana — somewhere in South America — that's fifteen minutes off. There are others, too. Meshed is eight and a half ahead of us." He pronounced the Iranian city's name with his more than passable Farsi accent. "I'm surprised you didn't know that."

"I must have. Yeah, I knew Newfoundland was an hour and

a half from us and I knew there were others. So, how you feeling?"

"I feel great. I found you a souvenir."

"You brought me a present?"

"Yeah. I'll bring it by the lab."

"Listen, I've been in here since 5 a.m. I need a break. Want to meet for lunch?"

"Yeah, I should eat on schedule so I get back on U.S.A. time."

"Denny's?"

"Of course. I just walked in the door; give me seven minutes to get it together and I'll head over."

"See you there."

Stevie lived close to Denny's (it was one of the reasons he chose the house he did — location, location, location), so Bill needed the seven minutes' head start. He grabbed his helmet and his backpack and headed out to his mountain bike. It was a beautiful New Jersey day, corn and tomato weather. Bill was trying to remember to breathe through his nose, and the air smelled terrific. He flexed his ankles more than necessary on the pedals just to feel the stretch. Out of habit, he glanced at his watch and then reached up to his neck and took his pulse. It was a game — he tried to count his pulse and guess when exactly twelve seconds went by at the same time. If he hit twelve seconds dead on, he would multiply by five and figure his beats per minute. If his estimate was off, the math got harder. He counted just under twenty-eight beats and he was a second over — thirteen seconds. 128.077 BPM, the last three places didn't mean anything, false accuracy, but his pulse was under 130 and that was pretty okay. He was pedaling hard. He wasn't in bad shape, fairly healthy, that's good.

Stevie didn't have to look at the Denny's menu.

"'Moons Over My Hammy,' that was the only English phrase that was going through my head. I was thinking in Farsi, I really was. But, man, I missed my 'Moons Over My Hammy,' it was literally the longest I've gone without them since 1982." Stevie loved his Denny's.

Bill just listened. Stevie knew the stories he was going to tell
and the points he was going to make; he'd worked it all out on the
airplane. Bill was Stevie's friend, and Stevie knew he was interest-
ed in the trip. Stevie didn't need to wait to be asked: it was more
efficient to just tell the stories. There was a story about it looking
like his visa had been revoked at the last minute and a funny story
about a strip search. The American government had been more
hassle than the Iranians. Stevie had traveled all over the Middle
East. "I love the geography, love the history, love the languages,
love the culture, love the people. I hate the religion and I hate the
government — hey, it's the same way I feel about North America.
But, believe you me, the worst here is a way lot better than the bad
there, a way lot better."

Stevie emptied two little plastic jelly containers onto a half
piece of toast. One was marmalade and one was the generic
"mixed berry" — a lot of sugar and weird flavors to hold even for
Denny's white bread.

"So, you remember Phyllis, you know, the ichthyologist
woman that I met at the conference in Diego two years ago? Well,
she got grants for another eighteen months in the jungle, and she
decided to stop off and visit me on the way."

"On her way to Africa, I guess, right? I mean where else is
the Middle East on the way to?"

"Yeah, well, Madagascar, it was kinda sorta on the way."

"You've been seeing a lot of her."

"Yeah, we get along well. But she got really goofy over there
though. I mean we still got along, but the Iranians made her crazy.
She bared her arms in public. She almost started a riot."

"I'll tell you, that was the first thing I noticed about Phyllis,
the woman has a bodacious set of arms."

"It wasn't funny; they could kill her for that — they'd kill me
too. They consider her my responsibility. They do. We had to act
like we were married to travel together. We wore rings and stuff."

Stevie had gotten through most of the important stories, and
Bill brought him up to speed on all the Lab gossip. There was a
lot of business stuff going on in management, but as long as one

still has a job, research is research, and even in three months, nothing important changes.

Stevie drank more than enough Denny's coffee to reset his biological clock and pulled a plastic bag from out of his backpack. It was a crumpled white "I ♥ NY" bag. "The guy who sold me this object gave me the bag. This is the bag he had. It really is one–world/one–people/one–culture. It's a one-company-that-makes-bags-for-cheesy-gift-shops planet. I had plastic bag carry-on."

"Oh, man, that's the worst. You carried this on?"

"Yeah, I did it for you."

"You did plastic bag carry-on for me?"

Stevie handed the bag across the table. "Go ahead, look at it." In the bag, surrounded by wads of Arabic newspapers (no pictures), was a beat up oil lamp.

Stevie was excited. "It's bronze. It's old. You'll be able to tell how old — a couple thousand years anyway. David can probably tell you exactly. It was hard to even tell it was bronze with all the crap on it, but it's bronze; I made sure of that. And I'm sure it's been around longer than the christ myth. It's also way illegal. That's why I carried it on — I've found they check checked luggage closer than carry-on. I told the customs guy it was a wrapped up ashtray: an American who knows the colloquial word for ashtray was enough of a novelty to misdirect. I bought the lamp from a really seedy guy in Meshed right at the end of the trip. Of course, everyone who sells anything to Americans in that city is seedy, but this guy was really seedy. He couldn't believe, with my accent, I was American, and I look damned American. He told me that it was from a recent desert dig way in the southwest, but I don't really trust anything he said. Stuff from digs is supposed to go right to the government, but bureaucrats don't know jack, so I snuck it out for you. I know how you love old bronze. When I saw it was bronze, I had to get it for you."

"This is amazing. I feel like the British Museum, like maybe someday, some way, I'll have to give it back."

"You know, don't feel bad about it, you know that govern-

ment, they'd just take it and melt it down for the copper and tin.
It does more good for the world in your hands. If you feel you're
bound by the laws of the Middle East, you're going to have a hard
time living your life. Pork and anal sex, even at different times, go
right out — no more 'Moons Over My Hammy.'"

"I have nothing in my collection that even comes close to
this. I don't know what to say. Jeez, Stevie, you never give gifts."

"I never give gifts on holidays and I hate getting gifts on holidays, but when it's the just right thing for a good friend . . . You're
a good friend, Bill; call it pay for watching my fish for thirteen
weeks."

That night Bill was in his home, in his collection room, and
he was reading the directions he'd pulled from the Net for cleaning bronze that had been buried in the desert. RTFM. He'd read
them enough to have memorized them. He had white butcher's
paper spread out over the table, two bright clip-on lights and a
magnifying light. The lamp was beautiful bronze workmanship.
He wasn't going to polish it, just get some of the caked crud off.
He wasn't going to do much. It was the perfect piece to just stare
at, to just be in the room with. He had a bell jar for it, and it
would sit on his shelf, in his collection room. He always read in
his collection room. It was his library. It had his chair. He read
every evening for over three hours, and reading in the room with
his bronze connected him to the technology and art that makes us
human. He had the blood of an archeologist, but he got paid for
research in computer operating systems.

He had taken several dozen digital pictures of the lamp, just
the way it came out of the white plastic bag and the Arabic newspaper. It was recorded from every angle. He would put the best
lamp pictures on his pre-christian web page. He'd get feedback,
people would be able to tell him a lot. He just wouldn't mention
where he got it.

He had a few lint-free cloths and a bottle of one-step-short-
of-homeopathic-dilution cleaner. He took an eyedropper and put
a drop on a corner of the cloth. With another cloth he held the
handle of the lamp. Stevie and the Iranian grave robber (that's a

great name for a situation comedy) would be the last two people to have their flesh touch this lamp as long as Bill was alive. From here on in, Bill would do everything right. Looking through his magnifying light, with his video camera trained on his hands, he gently turned the lamp over. There was a piece of dirt stuck on the bottom; he would start there. He touched it lightly with the cloth and nothing happened. He increased the pressure — nothing. He pushed harder, keeping an even pressure while staring and straining his ears for any sign of damage until the little piece of crud fell off into the waiting white cloth. He picked up the crud with tweezers — he could see no bronze. The piece of crud looked like it was 100% crud — good. The patch of bronze that showed though the grit looked perfect. Man, this was good workmanship. He took a clean Q-Tips brand cotton swab and rubbed the newly fresh bronze with an ever so gentle, tiny circular motion and . . .

Wam! Bam! Alakazam! Bill's hands flew off the lamp and over his head. He didn't move his hands over his head, something else did. His hands were up in the air and vibrating like a frightened maid in an Abbott & Costello ghost comedy. The lamp floated in the air. It hovered, not precarious like a superconductor on a magnet, but solid, like the Earth floating in space. The cruddy bronze lamp righted itself and trembled. Thousands of years of grime and crap fell onto the table and the bronze shone. It shone like freshly polished new bronze for a few seconds and then glowed like the center of a halogen light. White light, white heat. For several seconds there was deep THX show-off sound, sub-woofer rumble. When the sound stopped, all the lights blew out like candles and the video recorder was toast. Wow. The only light in the room came from the lamp and there was plenty of light.

Bill was not in shock. He couldn't move and he couldn't think, but he was taking in everything. The lamp began to release a bright pink smoke, which did not dissipate as it got farther from the lamp. It stayed together and moved with purpose. The smoke had an agenda. The pink mass floated in space and started splitting into component elements of different colors. A dark red guck emerged and began forming shapes, as the leftover brown and white began to condense into a human shape which slid around in space to encase the red entrails. It was no longer smoke: a swarthy, overweight, naked man now floated in a sitting position in front of Bill.

Bill began to get his body back. He relaxed his arms and opened and closed his hands. He moved his shoulders, legs, and neck around just to prove that he could. He looked into the naked fat man's eyes and had no intention of saying, "You're the genie of the lamp," but he said it. No intention to speak whatsoever, but he did, he had said it out loud. He hadn't thought the words before he said them, he hadn't felt the desire to speak. He heard the words only as he said them.

The genie nodded.

Now Bill spoke, on purpose, for the first time since the event. "You made me speak, didn't you? Is that your way of communicating? You'll use me? You'll make me talk and I'll listen to myself?"

The genie nodded.

He was forced to speak again. "I'll call you Spunky." Bill's voice, but the genie's idea.

The genie nodded.

"Spunky? Why Spunky?"

"That is correct. I'll call you Spunky because you think it's funny. It amuses you. It is your wish, and *I* will grant *you* a few easy wishes before you grant three difficult ones for me."

"Okay, fair enough, I guess. Jesus christ, this is weird. I'm talking to myself, right? I am talking to myself. Listen, this isn't a real wish, this doesn't count, okay? If it's going to count, you let me know and I'll take it back. This is just a favor: if you're going to have me talk to me for you, could you have me address me in the second person? You making me say 'I' about me is going to make me nuts. We have to talk, and it would be nice if you'd make it a little easier."

"Yes, I'm talking to myself, or rather you're talking to yourself — is that better? That wish doesn't count, but the next one will." Now Bill was talking to himself like a real nut.

The genie nodded.

"Question, not a wish — but, you, Spunky, the genie, are floating in front of me, I'm seeing that. That *is* real, right?"

"Oh, you're darn tootin' it's right!"

The genie nodded.

"'Darn tootin,' you made me say 'darn tootin'? How can that be? It's not a phrase I use and it's not a phrase that a mythical figure that's been in a lamp for three or four thousand years would use. What's up with that? Question, not a wish."

"We work in mysterious ways."

The genie nodded.

"Oh, so now it's first person plural — the 'genie we'?" So I freed you from the lamp and you are duty bound to offer me these three wishes, is that what you meant? — Not a wish."

"You catch on very quickly."

The genie nodded.

"What are the rules on the wishes? What are the parameters? Can I wish for anything? Clarification, not a wish."

"Three wishes and you can wish for anything you want. Anything."

The genie nodded.

"Question, not a wish — Do you go by what I say or what I think?"

"What you say."

The genie nodded.

"*Exactly* what I say, right? What I mean doesn't matter. No other rules? Not a wish."

"*Exactly*. No other rules."

"Good. You know, I've given this some thought." Bill took a deep breath. "First wish, this is a wish, it's one wish but it needs several sentences of explanation — I wish for your advice, with full disclosure. I will now clarify that wish. This is not a new wish, but the clarification of the one wish I'm making — what I mean by 'advice with full disclosure' is you will give me no advice that is in any way misleading and you will hold nothing back from me. I will clarify further, you will hold back no information, that you, in good faith, think I could use. It seems you can read my mind, at least a little, and you are to use that skill to make sure I understand everything you say perfectly. I wish to ask for your honest advice at any time I choose in the wish-making process."

"Okay, that wish is granted. You understand that you have two left."

The genie smiled.

"Advisor, will I be able to ask for an infinite number of wishes? Could that be a good thing for me and the world? This is not a new wish, this is just advice, part of the granting of the first wish."

"Well, if your wording is perfect, yes. And it could be a good thing for you."

The genie nodded.

"Okay, advisor, what is the wording I would have to use to get that wish just the way I wanted it?"

"'I would like all my wishes to be granted for as many wishes and for as long as I so desire on the deepest commitment from the genie of this lamp and the executive omnipotent, omnipresent forces of the unseen universe.' And you should probably add the end of that wish onto the first one."

The genie winced a little and nodded.

"Good, my second wish is for the first wish to be augmented with the second half of that phrase — I want your honest advice, as spelled out in the first wish, on the deepest commitment from the genie of . . . and so on."

"That is done."

The genie was disgusted. The genie nodded.

"Have I made any mistakes that I should clear up?"

"No."

The genie looked very unhappy but nodded.

"Okay, using the exact wording you advised for me to get an infinite number of wishes, please make that so."

"It is so."

There was one peeved genie nodding.

"So, Spunky, I have an infinite number of wishes, now, is that correct?"

"Yes," and the nod.

"I wish to have you consult with me, in good faith, *before* granting any wish. Is this wise?"

"Very, it is granted."

The genie scowled and nodded.

"Anything I'm forgetting?"

"No, it all seems covered in your plan — but you haven't added aloud that time should be stopped to give that advice. That way I can't have you run over by a truck while I'm advising you on the downside of wishing the truck not to run you over. There are also all sorts of careful parameters you're going to want to put on stopping time. We're talking all the *Twilight Zone* stuff."

Spunky really wanted to run Bill over with a truck, but the genie nodded.

"Make it so."

"It is so."

The genie nodded, with hate.

"Okay, the next wish. I want to stop talking to myself. I'll probably eventually just have you give me the necessary advice direct to my brain, but for right now, make it so smoke man is talking. And don't use a voice that sounds at all like Robin Williams."

"I'll grant that," said the genie with a dumb-ass Kevin Cost-ner California wimp voice. "The only disadvantage to that is it's less fun for me."

"I wish for you to ask me a second time before granting any wishes from now on, okay?"

"Well, to grant that wish within this system sets us up for a

Gödel logic problem, but I know what you mean. Want me to grant that wish?" The fat genie was very snotty.

"Yes, I do. Now, about your attitude. I don't think I want you to be surly. I wish you to love your job. And this situation. And I want you to like me."

"There is no downside to that for you, I'm afraid, but I'm going to hate liking you. Would you like that granted?"

"Yes."

"And perhaps you'd like me to look a little less like Buddha and a little more like Uma Thurman? And made of flesh. There will be no downside at all, unless you call a bit of an erection in the privacy of your own home a downside, and while we're at it, with all due respect, would you like your erection to be just a little more formidable — not grotesque, mind you, but just a wee bit out of proportion? And you're going to want to make sure that I advise you on downsides for other people and the world as a whole. Although you don't really need to use a wish for that, because if I were to hurt anyone else or the world, that would affect you, wouldn't it? So I'd advise you on that anyway, but you might as well spend a wish, you have plenty."

"Make it so."

"Are you sure?"

"Yes."

"It is so. Now, because I *can* read your mind a bit, I'm guessing my areola could be a little bit darker for your taste, a little more brown. Now, keep in mind that if you wish to make love to me, that you may find it less than satisfying, even a little depressing, because of the falseness of the situation, and a nagging memory of my previous form. No one has ever really done the sex-wish bit right, but . . . I bet we can find a way to make it pleasing. In the meantime, want me to darken up the areola and put a couple millimeters on the nipples?"

"Yeah, darker areola would be nice. Wow, and my penis is a little better the way you left it — good going. And, oh yeah, I'll have sex before the night is over, and I'm sure we can do better than you in drag. But let me tell you, you look as great as Uma. If she saw you, I bet she'd tattoo her nipples brown. And that, Spunky, is a great thought. I wonder if it's worth a wish."

They talked deep into the night. The wish thing was an interesting logic problem, and Bill enjoyed thinking, discussing, and experimenting. He wouldn't wish to lose weight, he would wish to have cravings for the exact foods that would be good for him and in the exact right amounts. He wouldn't wish for a fake Uma, nuttily in love with him; he would wish to know his best bet with the women he had met. In the meantime, he would have some wild fake sex tonight, just to hold him over. He'd do some other stuff he'd always wanted to do: he would feel what it was like to be weightless in space, and directly observe extinct cultures. And, slowly, almost imperceptibly, the world would become an even better place.

As dawn approached, Bill's brand-new digital video camera captured his cleaning of the lamp from a couple angles for the web. He smelled the clean old bronze and put it under the bell jar on the shelf. He opened a book of essays by Nicholson Baker and prepared to doze off in his favorite chair, in his library, in New Jersey. After a refreshing sleep and "Moons Over My Hammy," he'd be back at the Labs. He could just barely wait to tell Stevie about the elegant new technique he'd found for using some of their old networking code.

IF YOU THOUGHT YOU'D GET IN TROUBLE FOR SOME OF THE OTHER TRICKS, WAIT UNTIL YOU SEE THIS ONE!

THIS BOOK HAS SOME CUTE TRICKS. That's a fun little thing to do to a nosey neighbor on the airplane. Squirt soda all over. Break an airplane cup. Flush money down the toilet. But let's really raise the stakes. There's a chance this next trick could really send you to jail. Before you even read the trick, you need to know this: I wrote an inferior version of this trick for a cheesy computer magazine and the F.A.A. called them and then me and threatened to take us to court if anyone ever really did the trick or if it was ever printed again. We printed it again in the same mag the next year and we're publishing it again here. I've never *done* the trick. To my knowledge no one has ever done the trick. I don't know what would happen if you really did it. We think it may be our worst idea since the infamous Murtala Muhammed International Airport Impromptu Bullet Catch. You want to find out what happens to me if someone *really* does it? Ball's in your court.

If you believe that all the extra airport security is really making us safer, don't read any more of this article. Just skip it. If when asked, "Did you pack your own bags?" you're never tempted to say, "Well, no, actually a Middle Eastern gentleman came to my room this morning and packed my bags while I had breakfast," just forget the rest of the article. There are lots of good card tricks in the book that won't offend; you can go back to those. If you believe they've ever had one person answer that packing question in a way that helped them find a bomb, then go back to the soda can trick — it's a great trick.

I sincerely don't want to offend any of our readers, but I've got something to say. It's very simple, but a bit controversial: The United States of America does not have a problem with terrorism. We

just don't. It's not because of all invasions of privacy and wasted
time at the airports. The main reason we don't have a problem is
because, even *with* all those stupid checks, we still have a way lot of
freedom. More than anyplace else. When you're in a country where
you can say and do most anything you want, it's hard for a nut to
rally other nuts to evil nuttiness. Even nuts know enough to say, "If
you think the government sucks and is treating you wrong, why
don't you just go on some nut talk show and say so. They'll fly you
to a major city, pick up your hotel bill, and give you snacks in the
green room. That's better than blowing something up."

Add up all the terrorism that we've had in the United States
over the past ten years. More people have been killed by family dogs
(and that's mostly kids). Even one death in the history of the world
because of terrorism is *way* too many. It's unacceptable. But in this
country, we can stop terrorism with freedom. If you have enough
freedom, you have very little terrorism. In the U.S.A. we're working
hard not to oppress anyone, and the Constitution says we're supposed to let anyone say any damn thing they want.

The purpose behind terrorism is to bring about terror. Let's not
let it work. Let's keep things free. Let's consider those terrorism victims heroes. Let's say they died for freedom. They didn't die for us
to have our phones tapped and have our time wasted at airports.

I fly a lot. It's part of my job. I bring a laptop with me. Computers are the only thing I've ever really loved that I haven't tried to
destroy (maybe I'm sharing too much for a travel book). This prank
will not solve the problem of getting a computer through security
quickly or diminish your discomfort. In fact, it will increase your
problems, pain, and discomfort, but it will make other people suffer,
too, and that's even better.

I guess if you fly out of some Hooterville airport they just let
you walk through whistling the *Andy Griffith* theme with a few
pounds of hardware over your shoulder. But all the real airports
want to check it out. Security wants you to turn the computer on.
They want you to show them it works. They want to make sure
you haven't got a gun hidden in it. They're big crybabies. It's just

another pain in the ass as our society tries to live a "no risk is accept-able" lifestyle. Hey, we're alive, there's risk. Some planes are going to go down like falling twisted burning human cattle cars and there's no stopping it. No one can make any form of travel 100% safe. We'll take our chances. Let me walk through the airport without taking my bracelets off and turning my computer on.

Here's the bad idea. It's a pretty cool idea. If you do it, you'll probably go to jail and we'll get in big trouble. All they ask you to do at security is to turn on the laptop and show something on the screen. They just want to see it print something on the screen. (We all know that a bomb with a laptop taped on top of it could print something on its screen, so if this security check stops anyone, it'll be a way stupid terrorist that can score C-4 but can't get his hands on tape.) All they want to see is something on your screen. So let's give them something on the screen. Either set up your start-up screen or save a few screens that say the following and have them pop up one after the other:

READY
ARMING . . .
ARMED
0:17:00 UNTIL DETONATION
0:16:00 UNTIL DETONATION

. . . and so on . . . If you really do it, I don't know what will hap-pen. They probably won't notice, they're just looking for letters on the screen, they probably won't even read it. If they do notice, you might be able to convince them it's funny. But, like several of our tricks, it might also be a federal offense. I don't know enough about it. I did see a sign at an airport once that said, "All jokes will be taken seriously," which bad improv groups should read and take to heart.

They might want to make an example of you. The country loves to see a "computer nerd" in a suit holding cuffed hands up to obscure the guilty face. They'll probably call you the "Airport

Hacker," or "Terrorist Hacker," or "Militia Hacker," or "Prankster Hacker," but you *know* they'll get the word "hacker" in there, even if you never wrote a line of code. You know they'll force Cliff Stoll to make a statement. You'll try saying you did it because some magic boys in a travel book told you to. You'll try the ever popular "the-media-made-me-do-it" defense. The climate in the country is such that they probably would drag us in. But they won't have a thing on us, not after we do this:

DISCLAIMER

The above is not funny. Do not under any circumstances do what we've suggested above. It was just a joke. Penn Jillette, Teller, and all the employees and families of Penguin Putnam Inc. think that everyone in the world should really, truly, and honestly follow all federal and state laws and all F.A.A. rules, regulations, and suggestions. NO KIDDING.

So try it if you want but we're not going down.

THANK-YOUS

A list of people who were important to this book (34% of whom we'd take a bullet for).

T. Gene Hatcher and Kari Coleman — they know.

P&T are not just two people. We're a bunch of people. Ken Krasher Lewis runs our lives and our business. He's our benevolent despot.

Burt Bramlett and Wiley Bramlett build everything and make it work. If you've noticed P&T getting better, it's because of them.

Glenn Alai and Nathan Santucci do a lot of work that has to be done and no one wants to do, and they do it with gusto & cunning. What more could you want?

Krasher, Burt, and Wiley run a tight ship and they have a crew thanks to Christie Moeller, Alisa Moeller, Diane Balle, and Rick Oehler.

Stacy Creamer is the publisher suit and a fine suit she is. She brought us Jeff Freiert, who is so good, he even checked the bible verses and that can put you off your food.

You have to have an agent and a lawyer; we're lucky enough to have Dan Strone and Elliot Brown.

Everyone says we have the best web site. It's because of Maggie Ragaisis, Paul Nielson, Michael Solinas, and Rachel Pevtzow.

Lawrence O'Donnell, Jr. is Penn's senior adviser.

Steve Shaw has great magic ideas coming out his ears.

Howard Bone and Harry Blackstone, Jr., we'll miss ya.

David G. Rosenbaum, David Glenn, and D. Glenn Ross forever.

Gwen Akin, Nicholson Baker, Barbra Jo Batterman, Martin Breese, Eric R. Brouman, Lance Burton, Socrates Cherry, Chris Christ, Robert Corn-Revere, Sandra Cullen, Pauline Devito, Ab Dixon, Doc Dog & Las Vegas Tattoo, Resse Edwards, Tim Ellis, The Enigma, Mike Epstein, Joel Fischman & Bally's Las Vegas Casino, Michele Fitzpatrick, Martin Gardner, Gio, Giovanni, Michael

Goudeau, Beverly Gresham, Ward Hall, Charles Hardin, Paul Harris, Debbie Harry, The Hat Company, Docc Hilford, Stephen Holmes, David Huff, Kevin James, Aye Jaye, Tim & Leslie Jenison, Kevin King from Nashville, Mac King, Ken Klosterman, Kramer, Patty Kreke, Erika Larsen, Robert P. Libbon, Allan Ludwig, Elaine Lund, Tom Mullica, Georgia L. Maher, Jay Marshall, Daryl Martinez, McCarran International Airport, Billy McComb, Eric Mead, Sam Psoras, Bob Read, Lou Reed, Todd Ritondaro, Todd Robbins, Jim Rose, Mojo Royale, Samina, Short Line Express, Mr. and Mrs. Spawn, Nadine Strossen, Pam & Johnny Thompson, Randy Tigue, Amanda Walker, Michael Weber, Richard Wilson, Gretchen Worden, and A-1 Multimedia, 3337 Sunrise Blvd. #8, Rancho Cordova, CA 95742.

If you've ever been to Movie Night in NYC, it's likely you deserve a thank-you.

There's this thing called "The Jungle." It's a computer community. It's the future. It's our life. Our ideas start in "The Jungle." Glenn Alai, Steven Banks, Burt & Wiley Bramlett, Alex Bennett, Phyllis Bregman, Dino Cameron, Kari Coleman, Colman deKay, Chip & Grace Denman, Tony Fitzpatrick, Renée French, Marc Garland, Ron Gomes, T. Gene Hatcher, Carol Krol, Ken Krasher Lewis, Diane Martin, Rich Nathanson, Rob Pike, Paul Provenza, James Randi, Nell Scovell, David Shaw, Rich Shupe, Gary Stockdale, Steve Strassman, Colin Summers, Jamy Ian Swiss, Mike Wills. The Jungle will never forget Barry Marx.

Conspicuous in their absence: Our Lord Jesus Christ, His Holy Mother Mary, Our Father, The Lord of Us All, Jehovah, Jesus Christ, Yahweh, Sasquatch, His Blessed Mother, Mother Earth, Gaia, The Great Spirit, The Muses, The Holy Ghost, Bill W., Higher Power, Mohammed, Allah, Buddha.

A SMOKIN' MONKEY PRODUCTION

"There's nothing funnier than a smokin' monkey."
— BARRY MARX